A. L. COCHRANE

Effectiveness and efficiency

Random reflections on health services

THE ROCK CARLING FELLOWSHIP

1971

The ROYAL
SOCIETY *of*
MEDICINE
PRESS *Limited*

The Nuffield Trust

Reprinted in this format 1999, and published by
the Royal Society of Medicine Press Limited,
1 Wimpole Street, London W1M 8AE, UK

ISBN 1 85315 394 X

Printed in the United Kingdom at the
University Press, Cambridge

Dedicated to

H.B., T.B., G.J., and F.M.

and the population of the Rhonnda Fach

without whose help I would never

have got started

Contents

Acknowledgements

I am deeply indebted to all those who have educated, stimulated, and tolerated me; in particular I would like to thank Sir George Pickering who has carried out all these three functions for a very long time. In addition I am grateful to my colleagues at the MRC's, Pneumoconiosis and Epidemiology Research Units: I learned, and am still learning, a great deal from them. More recently, in addition to those mentioned in the text, I am grateful to Professor Brian Abel-Smith and William Laing, who tried to educate me about economics, and Dr L. Fish who tried to educate me about loss of hearing in the elderly. They are not, of course, responsible for any of my views.

Finally I would like to express my sincerest thanks to Irene Calford, who did all the typing. She alone can read my writing.

Foreword to the new edition

I read Archie Cochrane's Rock Carling Lecture *Effectiveness and Efficiency* the year after it was published. It changed my life. As a young clinician, I was already aware of my capacity to harm patients inadvertently by applying some of the lessons I had been taught, and I was trying to make sense of the various and often incompatible opinions of senior doctors about preventing and treating health problems. I am sure that it is a comment on me as well as my teachers that, six years after I had been let loose as a medical graduate, Archie's little book introduced me in an evening to the notion that research might be helpful in assessing who was most likely to be right. The book also helped me to understand that some kinds of research are likely to generate more reliable information than others. In particular, I learned that random allocation to comparison groups was important to reduce bias in comparing treatments. I felt as if I had been given a compass to help me negotiate a jungle of often conflicting clinical opinions.

The book was important to me in other ways too. As someone who had grown up with the National Health Service, I identified very strongly with Cochrane's reiteration of the decent principle of equitable access to (effective) health care. He also made plain that, although a first challenge is to assess whether particular forms of care are more likely to do good than harm, tough choices would be needed to decide how resources should be deployed among forms of care that were known to have beneficial effects. In addition, and very importantly, he emphasised the need to make proper provision for humane, dignified and thus effective care when no effective therapies were available. As was made clear in a collection of essays which was published to mark the 25th anniversary of the appearance of *Effectiveness and Efficiency*, my reactions to the book were widely shared (1).

For those for whom Archie Cochrane was an epidemiologist who pioneered the development of field studies of lung disease in coalminers, it may be rather irksome that his name has become far more widely known because of his writings and lectures about health services during the 1970s. It was in an essay published at the end of that decade that he issued the challenge which has led to the international collaboration which bears his name:

> "It is surely a great criticism of our profession that
> we have not organised a critical summary, by speciality
> or subspeciality, adapted periodically, of all relevant
> randomised controlled trials" (2).

The evolution of the Cochrane Collaboration has been described elsewhere (3, 4), and a great deal of information about it is available in The Cochrane Library and on the organisation's website (www.cochrane.co.uk). Reactions to the Collaboration among professionals have been mixed. Some have suggested that "It is a fair bet that if Cochrane were alive today, he would be appalled by the use to which his name has been put"(5); others that "The Cochrane Collaboration is an enterprise that rivals the Human Genome Project in its potential implications for modern medicine." (6) We will never know what Cochrane would have thought of the Collaboration named after him, or how he would suggest it might fulfil its objectives more successfully. I feel fairly certain that he would have approved of the way that it is taking advantage of electronic publishing to update and improve its systematic reviews in the light of new data, criticisms and the development of methodology for research synthesis.

Archie Cochrane might also have welcomed efforts to involve lay people in defining and pursuing research questions (7,8). Chris Silagy, who has played a key role in the evolution of the Collaboration, implies in his Introduction to this new edition of *Effectiveness and Efficiency* that the Cochrane Collaboration will fail in its mission unless people using the health services find the results of its work helpful. I agree with him. That is why active involvement of lay people in the Collaboration's work is very important.

There is one reaction to the Cochrane Collaboration, however, which I am confident Archie Cochrane would have viewed with particular satisfaction. In 1996, after welcoming the emergence of the organisation, the president of the Royal Statistical Society had this to say:

"But what is so special about medicine? We are, through the media, as ordinary citizens, confronted daily with controversy and debate across a whole spectrum of public policy issues. But typically, we have no access to any form of systematic 'evidence base' – and therefore no means of participating in the debate in a mature and informed manner. Obvious topical examples include education – what does work in the classroom? – and penal policy – what is effective in preventing reoffending? Perhaps there is an opportunity here for the Society – together with appropriate allies in other learned societies and the media – to launch a campaign, directed at developing analogues to the Cochrane Collaboration, to provide suitable evidence bases in other areas besides medicine, with the aim of achieving a quantal shift in the quantitative maturity of public policy debates". (9)

Perhaps we can look forward to learning the answers to the questions that Archie raised about the effectiveness of corporal punishment in preventing schoolboys smoking cigarettes!

Iain Chalmers
UK Cochrane Centre
January 1999

REFERENCES

1. Thomas H. 'Some reactions to effectiveness and efficiency'. In: Maynard A, Chalmers I, eds. *Non-random Reflections on Health Services Research: on the 25 Anniversary of Archie Cochrane's Effectiveness and Efficiency*. London: BMJ Books, 1997: 21–27.

2. Cochrane AL. '1931–1971: a critical review, with particular reference to the medical profession'. In: *Medicines for the Year 2000*. London: Office of Health Economics, 1979, 1–11.

3. Chalmers I, Sackett D, Silagy C. 'The Cochrane Collaboration'. In: Maynard A, Chalmers I, eds. *Non-random Reflections on Health Services Research: on the 25 Anniversary of Archie Cochrane's Effectiveness and Efficiency*. London: BMJ Books, 1997: 231–249.

4. Dickersin K, Manheimer E. 'The Cochrane Collaboration: evaluation of health care and services using systematic reviews of the results of randomized controlled trials'. *Clinical Obstetrics and Gynecology* 1998; **41**: 315–331.

5. Shapiro S. Book review. *Journal of the American Medical Association* 1995; **274**: 668.

6. Naylor CD. 'Grey zones of clinical practice: some limits to evidence-based medicine'. *Lancet* 1995; **345**: 840–842.

7. Hart JT. 'Response rates in South Wales 1950–96: changing requirements for mass participation in human research'. In: Maynard A, Chalmers I, eds. *Non-random Reflections on Health Services Research: on the 25 Anniversary of Archie Cochrane's Effectiveness and Efficiency*. London: BMJ Books, 1997: 31–57.

8. Oliver S. 'Exploring lay perspectives on questions of effectiveness'. In: Maynard A, Chalmers I, eds. *Non-random Reflections on Health Services Research: on the 25 Anniversary of Archie Cochrane's Effectiveness and Efficiency*. London: BMJ Books, 1997: 272–291.

9. Smith AFM. 'Mad cows and ecstasy: chance and choice in an evidence-based society'. *Journal of the Royal Statistical Society* 1996; **159**: 367–383.

Foreword

In 1971 the Nuffield Provincial Hospitals Trust published a Rock Carling monograph *Effectiveness and Efficiency* written by Professor Cochrane. This proved to be a seminal work and influenced thinking about the assessment of medical treatment and procedures worldwide; and the work itself was translated into four languages. The Trust twice invited Professor Cochrane to update his monograph with a view to reprinting it, but he preferred that it should remain unaltered to reflect his views at the time of its conception. To meet the many requests received each year for copies of the original monograph has proved impossible.

Following Professor Cochrane's death in 1988, however, the Trust decided that it should republish the original monograph as a memorial edition in tribute to this remarkable man. The Trust has included in this volume a brief note written by Professor Cochrane reflecting upon the monograph some two years after its publication; and the obituary written with such honesty by Cochrane himself. Finally, it is very appropriate that this edition will be published at the same time as Professor Cochrane's own life story, written in collaboration with Max Blythe.

Nuffield Provincial Hospitals Trust
1989

Introduction to the new edition:
The Post-Cochrane Agenda: Consumers and Evidence

Chris Silagy

Chair, Cochrane Collaboration Steering Group (1996–8),
Foundation Director, Australasian Cochrane Centre (1994–),
Professor of Public Health, Monash University and Director,
Monash Institute of Public Health and Health Services Research,
Monash Medical Centre, Melbourne, Australia (1999–)

It is a privilege to be writing the introduction to this new edition
of *Effectiveness and Efficiency: Random Reflections on Health Services*
even though I never met the man who wrote it. In fact, it is barely
seven years since, during a period of postgraduate study in Oxford,
I first heard of Archie Cochrane's name and work. However, my
life and thinking have been transformed in many ways as a result of
this influential book, and subsequently my involvement in the
organisation named after him that now represents the ongoing
legacy of his vision and ideas.

In a strange way I also feel a sense of familiarity and personal
warmth towards Archie Cochrane, the person. As I have come to
learn more about his life I realise we share some interesting personal similarities. Both of us have suffered from life threatening illness – in his case tuberculosis and porphyria, in my case
non-Hodgkin's lymphoma. The effect that these illnesses have had
on our thinking and research is profound; a theme I will return to
later. Cochrane's ideas have challenged the thinking of generations
past, present, and I dare say, future.

There is no doubt that the vision Cochrane so clearly espoused
of an effective and efficient health service in his Rock Carling
Fellowship monograph (1) is as timely today as when it was first
published in 1972. That his vision has had such a significant influence on the development of health services around the world in
recent years is hardly surprising, given the simplicity and intrinsic
virtue and sense of his ideas. As we approach the end of the century
the issues of equity, that Cochrane also drew attention to, are of

particular importance given the social and economic disadvantage that now pervades so many societies.

The living legacy of Cochrane's vision is now an international Collaboration which seeks to "help people make well informed decisions about health by preparing, maintaining, and ensuring the accessibility of systematic reviews of the effects of health care interventions" (2).

The Collaboration's survival and rapid expansion since 1993 is not only a tribute to people such as Iain Chalmers (who was the main catalyst in translating Cochrane's vision into reality) but a reflection on the goodwill and efforts of more than 5000 clinicians, researchers, consumers, policy makers and funders from over 50 countries, and the support of many organisations, particularly the UK NHS Research and Development Programme. Collectively, they have ensured that the Collaboration is able to deliver its product successfully: an electronic library consisting of databases (updated quarterly) of systematic reviews, controlled trials, and methodological articles about the science of systematic review.

The Cochrane Collaboration has achieved a great deal in a short space of time. There are over 500 completed systematic reviews, many of which have had a significant effect on health services around the world (3). For example, in Denmark, a Cochrane review which was unable to demonstrate any benefit of routine ultrasound examinations in pregnant women led to the National Board of Health withdrawing its recommendation that pregnant women have routine ultrasound examinations. In Mysore, India, an economist and civil servant used information from a Cochrane review to help establish benchmarks for evaluation of the National Blindness Control Programme. In England and Wales, the results of a Cochrane review suggesting that widespread use of albumin in patients with hypovolaemia, burns or hypoproteinaemia results in hundreds of excess deaths per year has led to calls for a moratorium on indiscriminate use of albumin. I can just imagine the grin on Archie's face that yet another entrenched health care practice had been challenged! There are countless other examples of the impact that Cochrane reviews are having not only on clinical practice, but also on health care policy, research, and education.

Whilst such achievements are encouraging and worthy of praise, the task at hand is far from over. There are still about 190,000 controlled trials identified on the Cochrane Controlled Trials Register which are yet to be considered for incorporation into systematic reviews. Furthermore, the number of new trials is growing at a rate of about 4000 per year. The Collaboration certainly has its work cut out. It will take at least the next couple of decades to simply catch up with the backlog of existing studies. However, I have no doubt that the Cochrane Collaboration will meet this challenge. During the seven years I have been involved with the organisation, I have come to the conclusion that nothing is impossible given the commitment and dedication of those who have agreed to contribute to this endeavour.

However, even if the Cochrane Collaboration achieves its mission, there is no guarantee that decisions made in relation to health care will necessarily take account of relevant evidence. The broader reform of health care systems to adopt a more evidence-based approach has certainly been pushed along by the existence and work of the Cochrane Collaboration, but the extent to which real changes occur in the way health care decisions are made will ultimately reflect the intensely human and personal interaction between the users of health care services and those who provide services.

Whilst strategies to change professional behaviour, infrastructure support and resources, political policies, and the economic environment in which health care systems operate are all important determinants of health care decision making, I would argue that the most critical determinant of whether or not Cochrane's vision for an effective and efficient health service is achievable in the next millennium will rest not with health professionals, researchers, or even organisations such as the Cochrane Collaboration, but with consumers. By consumers I mean those people who use health care services. It is the involvement of empowered consumers (either as individuals or as representatives of specific populations) in health care decision making that will be the greatest challenge to health services in the coming decades. I would go even further to suggest that this empowerment and involvement of consumers represents the natural sequel to the agenda that Archie Cochrane so eloquently described 27 years ago.

★ ★ ★ ★ ★

Despite the concept of a partnership approach between health care professionals and their clients, the power balance within such a relationship has tended to be very much in favour of the health professional "who knows best" and acts in the client's interests. Such a power imbalance has also been reflected in decisions made at a population level about the organisation and provision of services, as well as in the agendas that generate new health care research. However, the past few decades have seen this power imbalance become increasingly questioned, partly coinciding with the general rise in the notion of consumerism, accountability, and rights that have pervaded many aspects of modern society.

In health care, the rise of consumer involvement has also reflected the trend towards more formalized systems of medical ethics and a focus on health outcomes that takes account of subjective individual experiences rather than just strictly biomedical events. However, Hilda Bastian, a prominent consumer advocate, has argued that some of these internal changes within the health care system are probably not responsible for cultural shifts, but rather represent the product of the health care system trying to catch up with changing times (4).

Bastian argues that consumer involvement and activism in health care has a much longer history, dating back in some cases for several centuries. She suggests that one of the main driving forces behind the key role of consumerism in today's society is the growing importance of ready access to knowledge and information, which hitherto may have been restricted.

Consumer advocates are now being offered opportunities and self-help materials to train in critical appraisal skills and research methods, as well as in public speaking, advocacy skills, fund raising and dealing with the media. Programs such as Project LEAD (developed by the National Breast Cancer Coalition in the USA), the CASP project in the UK, the "Making sense of health care research" workshops provided by the Cochrane Consumer Network, and the Consumer Research Workshops run by the Consumers Health Forum in Australia are all examples of this.

There is good evidence that the impact of consumer advocacy, particularly when supported with appropriate skill development, can have a significant impact on health care policy. There are few who would argue with the power of the women's health and maternity care movements, the disability movements, and more recently the HIV/AIDS consumer lobby groups, in influencing health care policy, service provision, research directions, and distribution of funding in those areas. Similarly, there is a growing influence of consumer groups in relation to several common cancers (such as breast and prostate), heart disease, and mental health.

One of the major challenges facing the health care system in the next millennium will be deciding how to respond to the growth in consumer advocacy. I doubt it will be acceptable to rely on rhetoric to acknowledge the presence of the consumer movement or to provide only limited opportunities for its involvement within the system. Rather, it is likely that more radical shifts in orientation and control of health care systems will see consumers take increasing responsibility for the organisation, delivery and development of health care services within their own communities.

Models of community controlled health care are increasingly being adopted in various settings in different countries with some success. These models involve delegating responsibility for purchasing and managing health care services from government to community groups. For example, in Australia there are now over 100 aboriginal medical services under community control, while in New Zealand, the USA, and Canada a growing number of indigenous communities are assuming independent control of their health services. Provided that there are appropriate community group structures, together with sufficient supports and safeguards built in to such models, they probably represent the ideal approach to health care purchasing and community-level decision making. I am yet to be convinced that other options which provide opportunity for consumer input are anything more than tokenistic.

Even if our health care system can develop ways of involving consumers more effectively at a community level, the greater challenge is how to involve consumers at an individual level. Despite the interaction between consumers and health professionals, embodied within 'the consultation' providing an important opportunity for a partnership approach to decision making, this does not always develop.

Work undertaken by Wendy Rogers, one of my recent PhD students, has demonstrated that even though respecting patient autonomy protects the rights of patients to make decisions for themselves, it also presupposes that patients are capable of, or wish to have, autonomy, which is not always the case. Through a qualitative study of patients in general practice with low back pain and their treating doctor, she has been able to show that one of the key elements of a doctor–patient relationship is trust. This quality builds over the time of the relationship. It is crucial to balancing power within the relationship and is an essential prerequisite for meeting the interests of the patient within a 'patient-centred approach'.

I found it interesting that even though many of the 20 patients interviewed as part of the work of Wendy Rogers were involved in doctor–patient relationships where there was considerable sharing of information and involvement of the patient in decision making, not one patient ever questioned the 'evidence-base' used by their doctor. If her study were repeated in ten years' time I doubt if any patient would not raise questions about the evidence that underpins the treatment decisions being made as part of their care.

I think that the major change to involvement of consumers at an individual level in health care decision making will arise as a result of their increased access to the same knowledge and information that the professionals they deal with have access to. How this will alter the professional relationship in the long term remains to be seen.

Tony Hope described this emerging conjunction of the concepts of evidence-based medicine and patient-centred medicine during a recent Kings Fund series "But will it work doctor?", as the conjunction of a paradigm shift in health care with a Copernican revolution (5). I hesitate to suggest how best to describe the resulting scenario, other than in terms of the 'post-Cochrane challenge'.

Our health care system is not yet at a stage where it is possible to provide the necessary knowledge and information to enable consumers to make fully informed choices in all instances. Hope has described the current relationship between evidence-based medicine and patient choice in terms of a Venn diagram comprising three overlapping types of information (see Figure 1).

The goal of evidence-based patient choice should be to increase circle A and its overlap with circle C. By necessity this means

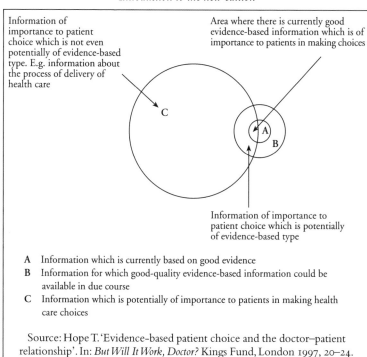

Information of importance to patient choice which is not even potentially of evidence-based type. E.g. information about the process of delivery of health care

Area where there is currently good evidence-based information which is of importance to patients in making choices

C

A

B

Information of importance to patient choice which is potentially of evidence-based type

A   Information which is currently based on good evidence

B   Information for which good-quality evidence-based information could be available in due course

C   Information which is potentially of importance to patients in making health care choices

Source: Hope T. 'Evidence-based patient choice and the doctor–patient relationship'. In: *But Will It Work, Doctor?* Kings Fund, London 1997, 20–24.

FIGURE 1. The relationship between evidence-based medicine and patient-centred medicine

greater involvement of consumers in identifying the type of information that is critical to making their choices. Researchers have a responsibility to try to generate such information, while health professionals involved in the provision of care have a responsibility to assist consumers in accessing, understanding, and applying the information that they need to make choices. Such a scenario highlights the importance of consumer involvement at every level within the health care system (from designing and funding research through to deciding what should happen about care provision within an individual consultation). It is a potentially threatening scenario to professional groups that have been used to determining their own agendas.

There are a growing number of examples of initiatives that are starting to address the conjunction of evidence-based medicine with patient-centred medicine. Firstly, many health care systems are now removing some of the practical barriers that have prevented consumers from accessing health care information and are even establishing specific consumer health information services. Secondly, a number of groups are now actively developing evidence-based patient information in a variety of easily usable formats, ranging from leaflets to audio and video tapes, and even interactive CD-ROMS. These resources can be tailored to different educational levels and varying individual needs. Evaluative studies of such materials have brought favourable responses from consumers who report that it assisted them with making their treatment decision (6).

However, there are dangers that could threaten the potential value of evidence-based patient information. With the rapid growth of content on, and access to, the Internet there is an unlimited world of information that consumers can now consult. Anyone can look for information in relation to a health care decision on the Internet, actively solicit advice and help from other consumers or professionals without the need for a formal consultation or assessment, and then order their preferred medication without ever leaving the front door by simply by pressing a few buttons on their home computer.

The need for reliable quality filters in relation to health care information provided over the Internet is critical (7). In addition, much of the Internet is driven by commercial considerations and advertising, with most of the big search engines designed to retrieve commercial sites in preference to not-for-profit sites. The training of consumers in search techniques and critical appraisal skills will be critical to ensure that they are assisted to use the Internet appropriately.

My recent personal experiences in dealing with non-Hodgkin's lymphoma have convinced me more than ever before that evidence-based patient choice ought to be a fundamental right of every consumer. Imagine being faced with an illness where there is little rigorous evidence to support high-risk treatment choices. As I write with my disease in relapse, I am trying to weigh-up the choice between high dose chemotherapy with autologous stem cell rescue against an allograft from an unrelated donor (since I am not fortunate enough to have a sibling with whom I match). The first option has a cure rate of about 20% and a mortality from the procedure of 3–4%. The second option has a cure rate of about 70% but a mortality of closer to 40–50%.

When one seeks reliable information to make such a major decision, surprisingly, there are no randomised trials comparing these two approaches. All these estimates are based on case series, which tend to select younger and fitter individuals. Few tell me what the likely side effects of the treatments are, and even fewer still tell me what my chances are of being able to kick a football with my sons after the different procedures. Furthermore, the data can only ever provide probabilities, which are often difficult to comprehend and, unfortunately, they can never tell me about what will actually happen to me.

Even though I have spent hours searching the Internet in the hope of some help, all I end up with are other individuals' experiences of different types of transplant, plenty of offers of alternative therapies for which great claims of effectiveness are made (and which I can order by electronic mail), endless lists of what new research studies have been published (but with no attempt to assess or comment on their quality or synthesise the results with previous research). Sadly, even when I search the Cochrane Library, I find that the Collaboration is yet to establish a Haematological Malignancies Review Group.

Fortunately, I am sufficiently educated to be able to wade through this information and synthesise what I can for myself. I am determined that no matter how much I trust my treating doctors I want to be assured that the decisions we make together are based on as much evidence as is in existence at the time. I believe that is my fundamental right, and a right of others in a similar situation. The challenge I face in getting the evidence I need to make informed decisions is almost overwhelming. I also believe it is my right to determine the value that I place on different outcomes, to express my own treatment preferences (and have these taken into account), and to feel that my treating doctors are prepared to respect my experiences as a valid and important input when we come to make decisions.

If I have learnt one thing from this experience it is to reinforce the crucial role that organisations such as the Cochrane Collaboration have to play in facilitating consumer involvement and empowerment in health care decision making. The Collaboration is an outstanding example of efforts to ensure that consumers not only are co-producers in the design and conduct of research, but also have the results fed back to them. This was one of Cochrane's strongest beliefs.

Although the Cochrane Collaboration is far from perfect, it has attempted to pay more than lip service to involvement of consumers. Not only are consumers represented on the major decision-making structures within the Collaboration, they are also expected to be an integral part of every Collaborative Review Group. Ideally, consumers have an opportunity within review groups to influence the agenda; to identify priorities for what areas ought to be reviewed, the outcomes that ought to be examined, the interpretation and implications that are drawn from the results. The Collaboration also supports an independent Consumer Network, which acts as a broad coalition of individuals and groups concerned with public participation in the organisation.

A recent survey of consumer involvement within the Collaboration (8) found 81% of collaborative review groups involve consumers in some way, and in 54% of review groups the involvement was greater than at the same time the previous year. However, with two exceptions, the involvement of consumers was limited to one country per group. Achieving true international consumer participation will require collaborative review groups to involve consumers from different countries, including those from the developing world. The survey also identified a number of other challenges with consumer involvement, that include providing appropriate support, resources, training, making materials accessible to consumers, spreading the load, and avoiding tokenistic involvement.

Probably one of the Collaboration's greatest contributions is the provision of accessible evidence-based materials to assist individual consumers in making informed choices. Although the organisation can't hope yet to meet the needs of every individual in every setting in every country, it is trying to ensure that its reviews, together with various derivative products (such as consumer synopses), gradually cover most of health care in a readily accessible format that is readable in different languages by informed consumers.

The Cochrane Collaboration in itself does not represent, or purport to represent, some future model for the health care system into the next millennium. However, it does represent an example of how the conjunction of evidence-based medicine and patient-centred choice can be actively supported at an individual level through its high quality, regularly updated, electronically disseminated products. At an organisational level it represents the type of commitment that health care organisations will need to be making to involvement of consumers at a broader level. What it has managed to achieve in the last seven years is a fitting tribute to Archie Cochrane's original vision, as well as being a beacon of hope that the post-Cochrane agenda of consumer involvement and empowerment in health care decision making is both realistic and achievable. For my own sake, and the sake of others like me, I sincerely hope it succeeds.

ACKNOWLEDGEMENTS

I am indebted to my colleagues in the Cochrane Collaboration for inspiring and guiding the development of my thinking over the past seven years. I am particularly grateful to Hilda Bastian, Iain Chalmers, Jenny Doust, Philippa Middleton, Wendy Rogers, Jane Silagy, Bronwyn Veale, and David Weller for their helpful comments and suggestions on this introduction.

REFERENCES

1. Cochrane AL. *Effectiveness and Efficiency: Random Reflections on the Health Services.* Rock Carling Monograph, Nuffield Provincial Hospitals Trust, 1972.

2. Chalmers I, Sackett DL, Silagy CA. ' The Cochrane Collaboration'. In: Maynard A, Chalmers I (Eds) *Non-random Reflections on Health Services Research.* BMJ, London 1997, 231–249.

3. 'Cochrane Collaboration'. *Cochrane News* (Ed: K Stamp), San Antonio, 1998, **4** (2), 1.

4. Bastian H. 'Speaking up for ourselves: the evolution of consumer advocacy'. In: *Health Care, International Journal of Technology Assessment in Health* 1998, **14**, 3–23.

5. Hope T. 'Evidence-based patient choice and the doctor–patient relationship'. In: *But Will It Work, Doctor?* Kings Fund, London 1997, 20–24.

6. Entwistle VA, Watt IS, Davis H, Dickson R, Pickard D, Rosser J. 'Developing information materials to present the findings of technology assessments to consumers'. *International Journal of Technology Assessment in Health* 1998, **14**, 47–70.

7. Jadad A, Gaghardi A. 'Rating health information on the Internet; navigating to knowledge or to Babel?' *Journal of the American Medical Association* 1998; **279**: 611–614.

8. Meredith B. Unpublished informal survey on consumer involvement in the Cochrane Collaboration (Presented at the 6th Cochrane Colloquium, Baltimore 22–26 October 1998).

I

Introduction

When the Nuffield Provincial Hospitals Trust offered me a Rock Carling Fellowship to write a book about evaluating the National Health Service, I was vividly reminded of my very first venture in this direction. It was when I was a medical student in London in the 1930s. The idea of a National Health Service (NHS) was not then the source of my greatest enthusiasm. Anti-fascist activities (and in particular Spain) headed the list, but the NHS ranked high. There was, I remembered, to be some rally about the possibility of a National Health Service in some London suburb, and I decided to go alone with my own banner. (I had some trouble even in those days in fitting into organized groups.) After considerable thought I wrote out my slogan:

All effective treatment must be free.

I had a deep inner feeling that this was absolutely right: although I doubt very much if I would have passed a viva on the meaning of 'effective'! The slogan, I regret to say, was a flop. The only person who noticed it damned me for having 'Trotskyite' tendencies, but I still thought it had something. The idea of reviving this adolescent inspiration thirty-five years later was an obvious one, and, although it has led me into some problems of definition, I have persisted with it. I hope my sentimentality has not clouded my argument.

I had been convinced for some time about the final form in which any analysis of the over-all result of the various activities in the NHS should be expressed. If we are ever going to get the 'optimum' results from our national expenditure on the NHS we must finally be able to express the results in the form of the benefit and the cost to the population of a particular type of activity, and the increased benefit that could be obtained if more money were made available. For many reasons I do not think such an approach is possible, even on a narrow front, at present, but I wanted to aim in the right direction.

There are two preliminary steps which are essential before this cost/benefit approach becomes a practical possibility, and it is with these two steps that I am chiefly concerned. The first is, of course, to measure the effect of a particular medical action in altering the natural history of a particular disease for the better. Since the introduction of the randomized controlled trial (RCT) our knowledge in this sphere has greatly increased but is still sadly limited. It is in this sense that I use the word 'effective' in this book, and I use it in relation to research results, as opposed to the results obtained when a therapy is applied in routine clinical practice in a defined community. Some people would like to use the word 'efficacious' for this measurement. This seems reasonable, but as I dislike the word I have not used it here. Between the scientific measurements based on RCTs and the benefit measurements at two levels of cost in the community there is a gulf which has been much under-estimated. Those patients participating in RCTs are nearly always selected from the general population of patients. Different strategies of management may be needed to achieve levels of effectiveness comparable to those reached in the RCTs. There is in addition the vast problem of the optimum use of personnel and materials in achieving these results. This covers not only problems of treatment, but also those of screening, diagnosis, place of treatment and length of stay, and, if necessary, rehabilitation. To cover all these varied activities I have used the word 'efficiency'. I would agree that it is not a very satisfactory index. It might, for instance, benefit from being further subdivided into its component parts. It could also be argued that some of these components, such as 'length of stay' have therapeutic associations. I hope others will deal with this neglected subject in greater detail in the future, but for my purposes, which might be described as short and super-ficial, 'efficiency' seems a suitable all-purpose index. So much has been published about cost/benefit analysis in relation to medicine on a superficial level, that this valuable approach is in danger of making itself ridiculous.

Having chosen two indices, 'Effectiveness' and 'Efficiency', and made them mean what I wanted them to mean, I soon dis-covered that they were only applicable to a part of the NHS. I see the NHS, rather crudely, as supplying on the one hand therapy, and on the other board and lodging and tender, loving, care. My two indices are very relevant to the former, but only to a limited extent to the latter. I needed another index with which to compare the two branches of the NHS and add a little humanity to my approach. Returning to my early enthusiasm for the idea of an NHS, I soon discovered what I wanted: equality. The difference in the medical care of the rich and the poor was sufficient to touch the hardest-hearted student in the 1930s. The word 'equality' in medical circles has been cornered too much by the medical politicians, but I hope to show that it has wider uses.

I must make it clear at this stage how I intend to fit this personally invented terminology into the general scheme of things. I do this without any intention of laying down the law in this verbal jungle. I am sure others will do this more competently than I can. My only objective is to make my terminology generally comprehensible. There are two words which are frequently used in two different ways. 'Care', for instance, is used in a very general way, as in 'Medical Care' which covers all activities of the NHS; alternatively it is used as a contrast to 'cure' when subdividing the activities of the NHS. I have accepted this dualism, but spelt the former with a capital C and the latter with a small one. Similarly with 'Efficiency'. It is difficult to avoid using this in a general sense as for instance 'the over-all Efficiency of the NHS'. I have used a capital E for this, and a small e for the more specific use outlined above. I have used the usual division of the activities of the NHS into prevention, cure (including diagnosis), and care. I have divided 'output' similarly, but added a fourth division, 'social'. I have devoted most of the space to an analysis of effectiveness and efficiency in the 'cure' section, because so much more is known about it. There has been so little work done in the 'care' section that I decided to discuss it under 'Equality'. Changes in the 'standard of living' of that side of the NHS may well produce such marked changes that the evaluation of 'care' is difficult until equality with the cure side has been achieved. I do not claim in any way that these three indices enable me to cover all the activities of the NHS. I have no ambitions in that direction. I only aim to use these indices to make some points about the NHS in which I am personally interested.

Having chosen my indices with some difficulty I started to write and found myself faced with a difficulty I had not expected. What I did not realize before I started was the trouble in which I should find myself in expressing personal opinions without worrying about 'bias'. This is my first, and probably my last, book, although I have published the usual number of scientific papers. In these, I would like to think I have made some contribution to the reduction of bias in medical measurements. Such measurements are particularly liable to bias because of the traditional use of hospital patients for investigations, and the importance of individual opinion in many diagnostic and therapeutic assessments. I have attempted over the years, by developing the use of unselected communities, and the study of medical error and its control, and by encouraging RCTs, to reduce these inherent biases. In publishing such papers I have inevitably adopted that standard MRC style of writing which passes for scientific English. There is a lot to be said for it. It is accurate, meticulous, and almost bias-proof. Personal prejudice is concealed. The only drawback from my point of view (and I suspect that of others) is that I find it almost unreadable. Unfortunately I have become so used to writing that way that I found expressing my own opinion, without detailed discussion of possible biases, nearly impossible. As a result on many occasions the book came to a halt. I was horrified, being relatively unknown, that readers might imagine that I was an experienced respectable physician whose opinion everyone accepts on sight. I finally decided that the simplest solution was to admit my biases in advance to warn my readers.

In general I am emotionally biased in favour of the idea of an NHS. The cause is probably the social injustices I saw in the 1930s. I have travelled very widely and believe our NHS to be the best of a very poor lot, but I view the NHS now rather as one would a favourite child who is showing marked delinquent tendencies. I lack some of the qualifications required to write a book of this kind. The most serious of these is, I imagine, the paucity of my experience of patient care and the atypical nature of the little I have had. Nearly all of it was during my four years as a prisoner of war in German hands which educated me in two very different ways. The first experience was in the *Dulag* at Salonika where

I spent six months. I was usually the senior medical officer and for a considerable time the only officer and the only doctor. (It was bad enough being a POW, but having me as your doctor was a bit too much.) There were about 20,000 POWs in the camp, of whom a quarter were British. The diet was about 600 calories a day and we all had diarrhoea. In addition we had severe epidemics of typhoid, diphtheria, infections, jaundice, and sand-fly fever, with more than 300 cases of 'pitting oedema above the knee'. To cope with this we had a ramshackle hospital, some aspirin, some antacid, and some skin antiseptic. The only real asset were some devoted orderlies, mainly from the Friends' Field Ambulance Unit. Under the best conditions one would have expected an appreciable mortality; there in the *Dulag* I expected hundreds to die of diphtheria alone in the absence of specific therapy. In point of fact there were only four deaths, of which three were due to gunshot wounds inflicted by the Germans. This excellent result had, of course, nothing to do with the therapy they received or my clinical skill. It demonstrated, on the other hand, very clearly the relative unimportance of therapy in comparison with the recuperative power of the human body. On one occasion, when I was the only doctor there, I asked the German *Stabsarzt* for more doctors to help me cope with these fantastic problems. He replied: 'Nein! Ärtze sind überflüssig.' ('No! Doctors are superfluous.') I was furious and even wrote a poem about it; later I wondered if he was wise or cruel; he was certainly right.

The second experience in POW life was very different. It was at Elsterhost where all the POWs with tuberculosis (most of whom were far advanced) of all nationalities, were herded together behind the wire. Conditions were in many ways not too bad. Through Red Cross parcels we had sufficient food; we were able to 'screen' patients and do sputum 'smears' but radiographs were very limited. We could give our patients bed rest, pneumothorax, and pneumoperitoneum. There was a French physiologist who was expert in 'adhesion-section', and thoracoplasty was a possibility. We knew our patients almost too intimately. We spent most of the day with them and at night were locked in the same building. We had to attend their funerals and I usually acted as priest. (I got quite expert in the Hindu, Moslem, and Greek

Orthodox rites.) I remember at that time reading one of those propaganda pamphlets, considered suitable for POW medical officers about 'clinical freedom and democracy'. I found it impossible to understand. I had considerable freedom of clinical choice of therapy: my trouble was that I did not know which to use and when. I would gladly have sacrificed my freedom for a little knowledge. I had never heard then of 'randomized controlled trials', but I knew there was no real evidence that anything we had to offer had any effect on tuberculosis, and I was afraid that I shortened the lives of some of my friends by unnecessary intervention.

In addition to my lack of clinical experience I lack experience in medical administration. The next period of my life was passed mainly as a field epidemiologist studying defined communities. This gives one an interesting, but possibly a worm's-eye, view of the NHS. If one makes repeated visits to the same community, one certainly gets an unusual insight into the working of the NHS, but it is no substitute for administrative reponsibility. In fact the only excuse I can offer for writing a book on a subject far divorced from my usual research interests is an ill-supported belief that all medical administration would benefit from a scientific epidemiological training.

In more recent years I have, it is true, drifted from relatively pure into 'applied' research; though the difference has never been clear to me. One cause was John Brotherston who met me, while I was in a very distressed condition, at London Airport. He, very kindly, tried to distract me by arguing the case for epidemiologists like myself taking an interest in the working of the NHS. I had heard such arguments before without them having much effect, but on this occasion, either because he was so eloquent or because I was so off-balance, I saw the point at last.

Another lead came from research in my own unit. I slowly realized the relevance of community epidemiology to the problem of 'screening' which was then becoming a *cause célèbre* at the Ministry. From this point I was led to the use of epidemiological techniques for evaluating medical care. Another took me into contact with the Nuffield Provincial Hospitals Trust, to whom I am deeply indebted for their help and understanding. I am particularly grateful for their tolerance about the time I was given to write this book but must even so apologize for the haste with which it was finally completed.

Yet another factor was my personal friendship with Dick Cohen and Max Wilson at the Ministry (now the Department), who guided my early fumbles in this newer field and provided me with much information, a little money, many contacts, and great amusement. Finally, I found I liked it. There is something extraordinarily satisfying in designing an RCT of 'place of therapy', writing the protocol in such a way as to avoid all the ethical pitfalls, persuading all the necessary people to participate, and checking to see that no one cheats. The result, when and if you get one, is relevant in a very satisfactory way.

Such is my background. It is clearly one likely to breed bias when dealing with medical treatment and medical care in the NHS conditions. In particular I believe that cure is rare while the need for care is widespread, and that the pursuit of cure at all costs may restrict the supply of care, but the bias has at least been declared. Having liberated myself in this way I have possibly gone to the other extreme and written a very personal view of the NHS. I have quite consciously concentrated on the bits that interest me and only sketched in the rest. I hope it is still readable.

The sequence of the book itself is fairly straightforward; after a historical sketch, and a brief look at the NHS there is a diversion to discuss the value of evidence in preparation for the discussion of effectiveness and efficiency in prevention, treatment, and diagnosis. The results of this section are then summarized before having a look at 'equality'. Finally, I have a look at the future, the possibilities, and the snags.

2

Historical sketch

There are three different strands to the story which have finally combined to produce the complex pattern of the present-day NHS. There is first of all the straightforward story of the ineffectiveness of medical therapy historically. The best account is given by McKeown and Lowe (1). It demonstrates very clearly how environmental factors alone were important in improving vital statistics up to the end of the nineteenth century and that until the second quarter of this century therapy had very little effect on morbidity and mortality. One should, therefore, forty years later, be delightfully surprised when any treatment at all is effective, and always assume that a treatment is ineffective unless there is evidence to the contrary.

The second is a completely different story, which has not been studied in such detail, of the layman's uncritical belief in the ability of the medical profession at least to help if not to cure. The basis of this was probably the doctors' ability to reduce pain, the general placebo effect, the tendency of many diseases to disappear spontaneously or improve with time, and the higher education and social status of the doctor in the past which possibly assisted him in alleviating hysterical symptoms. Osler also noted that 'a desire to take medicine is perhaps the great feature which distinguishes man from other animals'. This led slowly to the very widespread belief that for every symptom or group of symptoms there was a bottle of medicine, a pill, an operation, or some other therapy which would at least help. The doctor on his side was hardly to blame for aiding and abetting in the production of this myth. He very earnestly wanted to help. He had a fair number of drugs at his disposal and had read and heard a lot of suggestions that drug X helped in disease Y and that a visit to a spa helped in disease Z. There was at that time no known way of proving that a drug was effective, and a general acceptance on the part of the general population that death was inevitable and that when it came it was causally due more to divine intervention than medical failure. It was a reasonable type of welfare service. Although economically biased, it did not really matter as it was all so ineffective. It was almost a marriage of two minds—between the desire to help and the desire to be helped. When the 'panel' patient appeared, he naturally translated the tradition into a demand (almost a right) for a bottle of medicine, and the doctor, not unnaturally, acquiesced. The gradual appearance of effective therapies increased the status of the doctor and even shed some reflected glory on the other ineffective therapies. The extent of prescribing was still controlled, though not to the same degree as previously, by economic factors.

With this background it is not surprising that the advent of the NHS led to an original sharp increase in prescription particularly for appliances. The economic barriers were down, but the later introduction of charges seems to have controlled the rate of increase. Between 1951 and 1968 requests for pathology tests increased three times, X-ray units of work nearly doubled. The patient expected the doctor to do something to help him: the more the better. The doctor wanted to help and he could usually think of some new drug he had not tried (ably abetted by the pharmaceutical companies) or of some new diagnostic test (ably assisted by medical research) he had not tried out. The really surprising thing was that the explosion was not greater than it was.

The third strand goes right back to the nineteenth century when, for reasons that are still somewhat obscure, British science divided itself into pure and applied, and decided that pure research was 'U' and applied research 'non-U'. This division has had a very detrimental effect on large aspects of British life, particularly the industrial world, but medicine has suffered as well. The tradition was strong while I was at Cambridge. I remember being advised by the most distinguished people that the best research should be utterly useless. The importance of this to my present arguments is best illustrated by the situation when the NHS was introduced. This was a national organization which from one point of view could be seen as giving a blank cheque both to the demands of patients and the wishes of doctors. Most industrial organizations of comparable size would have had a large research section checking on the effectiveness of the service it was providing. In point of fact there was no research of this kind for about the first fifteen years of the life of the NHS.

Part of the trouble was that in 1948 medical research meant the Medical Research Council. Its reputation was (and is) deservedly very high indeed. Its foundation was on the principle that it should have 'the widest possible freedom to make new discoveries unhampered by pressures to give precedence to those problems which appeared at the moment to be of the most pressing practical importance'. The idea was excellent but there have been some unfortunate and unexpected side-effects. The MRC inevitably was biased towards the pure and opposed to applied research. I do not mean by this that it encouraged 'useless research' in the sense of my Cambridge days, but that it encouraged research that might in time illuminate a large field. It could at times be very liberal on the applied side, for example, the setting up of the Pneumoconiosis Research Unit, but there was an ill-defined line beyond which the MRC would not go. It is summed up for me by the phrase 'The protocol's all right, but this isn't quite the sort of thing the MRC does.' An apocryphal story claiming that 'the MRC investigated God-made diseases while others could investigate man-made diseases' used to circulate. I like it as it brought out the snob element in the ill-defined division between pure and applied research as interpreted by the MRC.

In 1948 the then Ministry of Health, with the staff it had, was very hard pressed in introducing the NHS apart from doing research. It relied on the MRC to do what was necessary. The MRC continued doing the sort of research it had always done so successfully and as a result there was practically no applied research. There was another difficulty which I feel I must mention. There was at that time a grave shortage of medical research workers willing and able to do the sort of applied research that was needed. I must admit that had I been approached by the Ministry of Health in the early 1950s to do that sort of research I would have refused. The MRC represented my idea of what medical research should be about. There were doubtless a few research workers more intelligent and more long-sighted than myself who might have accepted, but I am sure there were not many. The fourth was one of 'know-how'. Operational research techniques had been developed during the Second World War and would clearly have been useful to the Ministry but the technique had not then been extended in such a way as to be able to evaluate the effect of therapy. Fortunately there was not long to wait. The new technique made its first appearance in a publication about the value of streptomycin in the treatment of pulmonary tuberculosis (2). It was an important paper in many ways, but from the point of view of the NHS it enabled Bradford Hill (now Sir Austin) to introduce to the medical world the techniques of the RCT which added the experimental approach to medical research. Its importance cannot be exaggerated. It opened up a new world of evaluation and control which will, I think, be the key to a rational health service. Freud in his *Zukunft einer Illusion* put his hopes on the gentle voice of intelligence producing order out of another more general chaos. I believe the RCT, suitably applied, may have a similar effect in producing an effective, efficient health service.

3

The National Health Service

I once asked a worker at a crematorium, who had a curiously contented look on his face, what he found so satisfying about his work. He replied that what fascinated him was the way in which so much went in and so little came out. I thought of advising him to get a job in the NHS, it might have increased his job satisfaction, but decided against it. He probably got his kicks from a visual demonstration of the gap between input and output. A statistical demonstration might not have worked so well. This is perhaps an unfair introduction to a serious and interesting problem, the input/output problem of the NHS, but it makes the right point in one respect. There are three different types of output from the NHS, though they do, of course, overlap. There is the social output in which the most important factor is the freedom from worry about the cost of medical treatment and care. Another factor is the increased equality between social classes and between different parts of the country, which I discuss later. Then there is the output in the form of improved care for those who cannot look after themselves. Neither of these lend themselves to detailed input/output studies but the third type of output, the 'cure' or 'therapeutic' output, can to some extent be looked at in this way. I am, therefore, concentrating on this aspect, not because I think cure is more important than care, but because I suspect there is a gross discrepancy between input and output in this sphere which needs investigating, and for which the information is beginning to become available.

I want to make it clear that no detailed input/output analyses are possible at this stage, but I do believe that a very crude analysis is worthwhile, and hope to demonstrate this. The first factor to look at is the 'external input'. This is the result of medical and other research which is of use to the NHS in carrying out its objectives. The NHS cannot claim any credit for this 'external' input. It can only be judged by the use that is made of it. During the life of the

TABLE 3.1. *Changes in various aspects of 'input' in the NHS*

	1959	1961	1963	1965	1967	1969
Hospital medical staff	16,033	16,932	17,971	18,905	20,395	22,001
Hospital nursing staff	190,946	200,458	215,219	232,310	252,509	262,644
Hospital professional and technical staff	21,878	23,404	25,377	27,814	30,681	33,245
General medical practitioners	22,901	22,218	22,159	21,489	21,293	21,505
Prescriptions (millions)	214·0	205·0	205·5	244·3	271·2	264·2
Pathology requests (thousands)	17,267	20,603	24,930	28,562	33,360	38,792
Radiology (units of treatment) (thousands)	21,126	22,481	25,121	27,704	30,209	33,881

Source. Extracted from Table 3.2, *Digest of Health Statistics* (Department of Health and Social Security, 1970) and personal communication (Welsh Office).

NHS this sort of input has been greater than in any other comparable period in history. Although penicillin was introduced before 1948, its extensive use belongs to this period. All the antituberculous drugs, the hypotensive drugs, cortisone, the antidepressants, etc., are also external inputs of this period; to say nothing of such important discoveries as polio vaccine. The list is not complete, but sufficient to establish the point that, other things being equal, one would have expected a very considerable output from the therapeutic side of the NHS because of the magnificent quality of 'external input'.

Turning now to the actual 'input' of the NHS, I want first to argue that in relation to our *per capita* Gross National Product (GNP) we spend a reasonable percentage (4 per cent in 1968) of our GNP on the NHS. This is not as high as some countries, but is not unreasonable. The next point I want to establish is that, in addition to spending a reasonable and increasing percentage of our GNP on the NHS, we have, since the start of the NHS, been employing more doctors, nurses, and other personnel, doing more diagnostic tests, prescribing more drugs, etc. Some of this is summarized in Table 3.1. In addition to the external input there has clearly been a very considerable increase in 'internal input', so a marked increase in output could be expected.

TABLE 3.2. *Expectation of life. Home population*

Age	Sex	1948–50	1957–9	1965–7
0	M	66·3	68·0	68·7
	F	71·0	73·7	74·9
5	M	64·2	65·0	65·4
	F	68·4	70·4	71·3
15	M	54·6	55·2	55·6
	F	58·7	60·6	61·5
25	M	45·3	45·8	46·1
	F	49·4	50·9	51·7
35	M	36·0	36·2	36·5
	F	40·1	41·2	42·0
45	M	27·0	27·0	27·2
	F	30·9	31·9	32·6
55	M	18·8	18·6	18·8
	F	22·4	23·1	23·8
65	M	12·2	12·0	12·0
	F	14·6	15·2	15·8
75	M	7·2	7·1	7·2
	F	8·5	8·8	9·3
85	M	4·2	4·2	3·9
	F	4·8	4·7	4·9

Source. Table 1.6, *Digest of Health Statistics for England and Wales
1970* (Department of Health and Social Security).

The crude approach to output is to look at changes in morbidity
and mortality over the period during which the NHS has been
active. Table 3.2 shows the changes in expectation of life over this
period. This gives a gloomy picture indeed, particularly for males,
but it is, of course, a very unfair one. The NHS cannot be blamed
if there has been an increased incidence of a disease for which there
is no effective means of prevention or treatment, although, of
course, it could be criticized if it were using ineffective preventive
or therapeutic measures in such cases. The picture is clarified a
little by the use of Standardized Mortality Ratios (SMRs) for some
individual diseases (Table 3.3) which show, for instance, how the
lack of change in expectation of life is due to losses on the
roundabouts being balanced by gains on the swings. The fall in
the SMRs for tuberculosis and some other diseases has been
balanced by the increase in the SMRs for ischaemic heart disease
and carcinoma of the bronchus. This makes it clear that no
approach can be made to the problem of output through mortality

TABLE 3.3. *Standardized Mortality Ratios (base-year 1968 = 100) for selected causes of death, 1959–69, in England and Wales*

Cause of death	Sex	1959	1961	1963	1965	1967	1969
Tuberculosis of respiratory	M	228	191	170	123	108	76
system	F	214	188	142	121	115	68
Malignant neoplasm of							
cervix uteri	F	110	106	104	102	101	99
Thyrotoxicosis with or	M	260	195	142	179	188	206
without goitre	F	156	147	134	107	108	86
Hypertensive heart disease	M	173	159	142	117	103	100
	F	181	171	150	118	101	96
Peptic ulcer	M	125	115	110	97	90	96
	F	110	105	108	88	96	99
Appendicitis	M	220	180	146	134	106	96
	F	166	170	149	133	107	96
Malignant neoplasm of	M	84	88	93	97	99	102
trachea, bronchus, and lung	F	63	72	78	86	96	102
Malignant neoplasm of breast	M	83	106	91	102	113	99
	F	92	96	97	97	101	103
Diabetes mellitus	M	70	83	85	88	89	101
	F	82	97	91	99	95	101
Ischaemic heart disease	M	83	89	98	98	95	100
	F	90	95	100	93	94	98
Venous thrombosis and	M	57	69	82	87	100	103
embolism	F	56	70	83	87	96	104
Cirrhosis of liver	M	91	106	99	100	92	105
	F	94	98	93	96	96	109

Source. Extracted from Table 9, *Registrar-General's Statistical Review of England and Wales 1969*, Part 1.

rates without a very detailed study of whether effective means are available for prevention or treatment, how efficiently they have been applied, and what ineffective methods are in use for each individual disease. It is worth stressing for instance that even if there were a fall in the SMR for a disease, unless it is causally related to preventive or therapeutic action taken by the NHS it cannot be put to its credit. The decreased SMR for carcinoma of the cervix might be considered such a case.

The morbidity data is much less reliable than the mortality data. The only comprehensive data is for employed males in the form of 'certified sickness'. Table 3.4 shows the changes since 1954.

The picture is a depressing one. There is no doubt that 'certified time lost' is increasing even when standardized for age and that this is a real output of the NHS as it is 'time off' certified by

TABLE 3.4. *Certified sickness absence for males in Great Britain standardized for age*

Year	Days per 100 men	Year	Days per 100 men
1954	1,279	1966	1,481
1960	1,277	1967	1,632
1965	1,516		

Source. Extracted from Table 62, *Social Trends* (1970).

Note. 'Certified days sick' are underestimated for the insured population by those men on Unemployment Benefit rather than on Sickness Benefit. The 'days sick' are underestimated further as no account is taken of periods of sickness less than that required for certification.

doctors under contract to the NHS. The first thing to do is to get this 'certified time off' into proportion and an obvious comparison is with time lost by strikes, about which we have all heard a great deal from both political parties as a threat to our national economy. The crude ratio of days lost from certified sickness/days lost from strikes is about 100 : 1 (Table 3.5), so it appears superficially that if strikes are a threat to our economy the NHS must be a disaster. However there are innumerable snags in the comparison. For instance the Department of Employment does not differentiate between men and women in industrial disputes, while the data for sickness absence is unreliable for women; sickness absence figures refer to Great Britain while strike figures refer to the UK, etc. All these points and many others are made in *Off Sick*, a publication by the Office of Health Economics (3). There are further difficulties in comparing the economic effects of the two different ways of losing a day's work. The strike causes a severe localized dislocation with a marked effect on output, while sickness if it continues at a regular pace has less effect. The conclusion is therefore that the two figures cannot be accurately compared and that the disaster, though still considerable, is less than it at first appears.

It is possible to do a breakdown of certified sickness by individual diseases, but the categories are much more unreliable than in mortality data (Table 3.6). This reveals the important point that when there are really effective preventive measures and/or effective therapy there has been a definite drop in time lost, for example, tuberculosis and dermatology.

TABLE 3.5. *Days lost due to certified illness (for Great Britain) and industrial disputes (for UK), 1959–68 (males and females)*

Year	Total days of certified sickness in Great Britain (thousands)	Working days lost due to industrial disputes in UK (thousands)	Ratio
1959	282,490	5,270	54/1
1960	274,930	3,024	91/1
1961	278,950	3,046	92/1
1963	288,860	1,755	165/1
1964	286,950	2,277	126/1
1965	299,240	2,925	102/1
1966	311,470	2,398	130/1
1967	301,130	2,787	108/1
1968	327,580	4,690	70/1

Sources. Department of Health and Social Security: *Digest of Health Statistics 1969*, Table 12.5; *Digest of Health Statistics 1970*, Table 12.3. *Department of Employment Gazette*, August 1971, Table 133.

TABLE 3.6. *Comparison between 1954/5 and 1967/8 in terms of spells of sickness commencing and total days of incapacity, standardized with equivalent 1951 population. Selected causes where a trend was present. Males only (percentage)*

	Days	Spells
Rises 1954/5 to 1967/8		
Sprains and strains	+267	+228
Nervousness, debility, and headache	+189	+139
Psychoneuroses and psychoses	+152	+ 68
Displacement of intervertebral disc	+147	+171
All injuries and accidents	+ 72	+109
Falls 1954/5 to 1967/8		
Anaemias	− 12	+ 2
Asthma	− 24	− 6
Skin diseases	− 24	− 30
Appendicitis	− 32	− 41
Pleurisy	− 44	− 36
Respiratory tuberculosis	− 83	− 74

Source. Extracted from Table 1 of *Off Sick* (3).

TABLE 3.7. *Net weekly income at work and out of work (married couple with two children under the age of 11)*

	1951	1960	1964	1968
(a) At work (average earnings for adult male manual workers in manufacturing, etc., industries and including Family Allowance and less National Insurance and tax)	£8·24	13·95	16·72	20·03
(b) Out of work (Sickness or Unemployment Benefit not subject to tax and including Earnings Related Supplement where applicable and Family Allowance)	£2·97	5·50	7·45	14·92
(b) As percentages of (a)	36·0	39·4	44·6	74·5

Source. Extracted from Table XI of *Social Trends* (1970) (converted to decimal system).

I hasten to make it clear that I do not think that my colleagues are entirely to blame for all this increase. They are facing a rapidly changing situation in attitude to work and lay knowledge of medicine. The change in the percentage of wages received as benefit when 'off sick' has changed dramatically (Table 3.7). They have my sympathy, in particular because I was once on the other side. For some time I was the only POW medical officer to a 'punishment area' near Wittenburg. Everyone was supposed to work particularly hard and discipline was very strict indeed, both for us and the Germans. The German MO knew that if he were caught allowing any malingering he would be sent to the Eastern Front. In spite of this I found it perfectly possible to quadruple the number of people 'off sick' at the sick parade. The POWs were carefully trained, and I specialized in the headache–migraine syndrome and back-ache. I used the French rather than the British as they were better actors. I also stage-managed small epidemics of mumps and acute nephritis. No one was ever shot or punished as a malingerer. I do, therefore, realize how difficult it is for my colleagues in general practice, as I note that the two groups of diseases showing the biggest rise (Table 3.6) are the two areas on which I specialized: 'headache' and 'sprains and strains'. I apologize to any GP who may be treating anyone I trained.

I do, however, think that the present situation should not be allowed to continue. There appear to be two solutions. Doctors could either cease to certify 'time off'; instead they would only advise. Alternatively they could undertake a major educational programme to help people understand the difference between the need for rest for therapeutic reasons or because of disability and the desire for a holiday. For the latter GPs would need shorter lists and better personal relations with their patients. To many patients in many industries there are slight financial advantages in being 'sick' and until this incentive is removed progress will be slow. A certain amount of standardization of length of time off for particular conditions by GPs would stop the practice of patients shopping around to find a GP willing to give the maximum time off.

This brief survey of the difficulties of using mortality and morbidity indices to get some estimate of the relationship between increased input and increased output proves little. It gives no information about the relationship between input and output before the period started as compared with during the period, and gives only suggestive evidence during the NHS period, but I do think there is sufficient evidence to justify a closer look at the effectiveness of some of the therapies in use in the NHS and the efficiency with which they are applied. Before doing this, however, I want to introduce a chapter on the value of different types of evidence, because this is crucial in assessing effectiveness and efficiency. There still seems to be considerable misunderstanding amongst the general public and some medical people about the relative value of opinion, observation, and experiment in testing hypotheses.

4

Evaluation of evidence

Two of the most striking changes in word usage in the last twenty years are the upgrading of 'opinion' in comparison with other types of evidence, and the downgrading of the word 'experiment'. The upgrading of 'opinion' has doubtless many causes, but one of the most potent is, I am sure, the television interviewer and producer. They want everything to be brief, dramatic, black and white. Any discussion of evidence is written off as lengthy, dull, and grey. I have seldom heard a television interviewer ask anyone what his evidence was for some particular statement. Fortunately it does not usually matter; the interviewers only want to amuse (hence the interest in pop singers' views on theology), but when they deal with medical matters it can be important.

The fate of 'experiment' is very different. Its current meaning, according to the *OED* and normal scientific use, is 'to test a hypothesis'. It has been taken over by journalists and debased from its usual meaning and is now being used in its archaic sense of 'action of trying anything', hence the endless references to 'experimental' theatres, art, architecture, and schools. (Someone once told me of a notice pinned to a church door referring to 'experimental' baptism. I spent a happy half-hour designing trials to measure the relative baptismal effectiveness of waters from the Jordan, the Tweed, and the Taff.) This misuse of 'experiment' has, I think, altered people's attitudes to observational and experimental evidence.

The general scientific problem with which we are primarily concerned is that of testing a hypothesis that a certain treatment alters the natural history of a disease for the better. The particular problem is the value of various types of evidence in testing the hypothesis. The oldest, and probably still the commonest form of evidence proffered, is clinical opinion. This varies in value with the ability of the clinician and the width of his experience, but its value must be rated low, because there is no quantitative measurement, no attempt to discover what would have happened if the patients had had no treatment, and every possibility of bias affecting the assessment of the result. It could be described as the simplest (and worst) type of observational evidence.

Moving up the scale at the observational level, the main changes introducing improvement are the appearance of 'comparison' groups, the introduction of measurement and the exclusion of possible bias from the measurements. Comparison groups as they appear in the literature are a very mixed lot. Some are positively grotesque, such as that old favourite 'those who refused treatment'. They are usually very different from the theoretical 'control' group, which should be the same in all respects, which might influence the course of the disease, as the treated group. This, of course, puts a limit on the possible accuracy of this sort of investigation as we seldom if ever know all the characteristics that might influence the course of the disease.

The best index in these sort of comparisons is the fact of death, where there is little possibility of bias due to observer difference, but whenever other measurements are made steps have to be taken to be sure the measurements have been made without knowledge of which person has been treated. But even with all these sophistications observational evidence is never very satisfactory. An example comes from Palmer's work in my own unit investigating a rather different form of therapy (4). He took very detailed smoking histories from all the boys in a secondary modern school on two occasions, one year apart. He then obtained a list of all the boys who had been caned for smoking during that period. He was thus able to compare 'change in smoking habit' in caned and un-caned boys (Table 4.1). The results appear at first very striking. Those caned increased their cigarette consumption significantly more than those who were not caned, but when one thinks about it the results do not tell us anything at all. They are equally compatible with caning increasing, decreasing, or having no effect on cigarette consumption.

Observational evidence is clearly better than opinion, but it is thoroughly unsatisfactory. All research on the effectiveness of therapy was in this unfortunate state until the early 1950s. The only exceptions were the drugs whose effect on immediate

TABLE 4.1. *Change brought about in smoking habits of schoolboys by caning, 1961–2*

	Increase	Change in smoking habit Same	Decrease	Total	X^2(2 df)
Caned	8 (35%)	10 (43%)	5 (22%)	23 (100%)	All caned *v.* All uncaned
Uncaned	10 (8%)	82 (67%)	31 (25%)	123 (100%)	12·9 ($P < 0·01$)

Source. Modified from J. W. Palmer's Table IV (4).

mortality were so obvious that no trials were necessary, such as insulin, sulphonamide, and penicillin.

The critical step forward which brought an experimental approach into clinical medicine can be variously dated. As previously mentioned I personally like to associate it with the publication in 1952 by Daniels and Hill (2). At any rate there is no doubt that the credit belongs to Sir Austin Bradford Hill. He has been much honoured but I doubt if we honour him enough. His ideas have only penetrated a small way into medicine, and they still have to revolutionize sociology, education, and penology. Each generation will, I hope, respect him more. (My pet idea is that there should be a 'Bradford' awarded to the best medical statistical paper of the year!)

The basic idea, like most good things, is very simple. The RCT approaches the problem of the comparability of the two groups the other way round. The idea is not to worry about the characteristics of the patients, but to be sure that the division of the patients into two groups is done by some method independent of human choice, i.e. by allocating according to some simple numerical device such as the order in which the patients come under treatment, or, more safely, by the use of random numbers. In this way the characteristics of the patients are randomized between the two groups, and it is possible to test the hypothesis that one treatment is better than another and express the results in the form of the probability of the differences found being due to chance or not.

The RCT is a very beautiful technique, of wide applicability, but as with everything else there are snags. When humans have to make observations there is always a possibility of bias. To reduce this possibility a modification has been introduced: the 'double-blind' randomized trial. In this neither the doctor nor the patients know which of the two treatments is being given. This eliminates the possibility of a great deal of bias, but one still has to be on one's guard.

There are other snags: first a purely statistical one. Many research units carry out hundreds of these so-called tests of significance in a year and it is often difficult to remember that, according to the level of significance chosen, 1 in 20 or 1 in 100 will be misleading. Another snag has been introduced by the current tendency to put too much emphasis on tests of significance. The results of such tests are very dependent on the number in the groups. With small numbers it is very easy to give the impression that a treatment is no more effective than a placebo, whereas in reality it is very difficult indeed to exclude the possibility of a small effect. Alternatively, with large numbers it is often possible to achieve a result that is statistically significant but may be clinically unimportant. All results must be examined very critically to avoid all the snags.

Another snag is that the technique is not always applicable for ethical reasons. There is, of course, no absolute medical ethic but the examples I quote here represent the majority of medical opinion at present, though I do not necessarily agree with them myself. They are: surgery for carcinoma of the lung, cytological tests for the prevention of cervical carcinoma, and dietetic therapy for phenylketonuria. No RCTs have ever been carried out to test the value of these standard therapies and tests. In the first two cases the RCT technique was not available when the surgical and medical innovations were made for carcinoma of the lung and cervix. By the time such RCTs were considered by medical scientists the one-time 'innovations' were embedded in clinical practice. Such trials would necessarily involve denying the routine procedure to half a group of patients and at this stage are nearly always termed unethical. It can be argued that it is ethically questionable to use on patients a procedure whose value is un-known, but the answer is that it is unethical not to do so if the patient will otherwise die or suffer severe disability and there is no alternative therapy. Such trials, it must be accepted, cannot be done in areas where the consensus of medical opinion is against them. This means, on the one hand, that patients' interests are very well protected and on the other that there are sections of medicine whose effectiveness cannot at present be measured and which, *in toto*, probably reduce the over-all efficiency of the NHS.

There are other limitations on the general applicability of the RCT. One important area is the group of diseases where improvement or deterioration has to be measured subjectively. It was hoped that the double-blind modification would avoid this trouble, but it has not been very successful in, say, psychiatry. Similarly the assessment of the 'quality of life' in such trials has proved very difficult. A good example is the various forms of treatment attempted for recurrences after operation for carcinoma of the breast. We have so far failed to develop any satisfactory way of measuring quality. Another area is relatively unimportant but worth mentioning: the rare diseases. Here the problem is the scarcity. For instance, in one case of porphyria variegata, in one acute attack renal dialysis appeared to be life-saving. In the next two it had no effect. It would need co-operation from most countries in Europe to complete a trial of this condition in a reasonable time.

Another very different reason for the relatively slow use of the RCT in measuring effectiveness is illustrated by its geographical distribution. If some such index as the number of RCTs per 1,000 doctors per year for all countries were worked out and a map of the world shaded according to the level of the index (black being the highest), one would see the UK in black, and scattered black patches in Scandinavia, the USA, and a few other countries; the rest would be nearly white. It appears in general it is Catholicism, Communism, and underdevelopment that appear to be against RCTs. In underdeveloped countries this can be understood, but what have Communism and Catholicism against RCTs? Is authoritarianism the common link, or is Communism a Catholic heresy? Whatever the cause this limitation to small areas of the world has certainly slowed down progress in two ways. There are too few doctors doing the work and the load on the few is becoming too great. An RCT is great fun for the co-ordinator but can be very boring for the scattered physicians filling in the forms.

In writing this section in praise of the RCT I do not want to give the impression that it is the only technique of any value in medical research. This would, of course, be entirely untrue. I believe, however, that the problem of evaluation is the first priority of the NHS and that for this purpose the RCT is much the most satisfactory in spite of its snags. The main job of medical administrators is to make choices between alternatives. To enable them to make the correct choices they must have accurate comparable data about the benefit and cost of the alternatives. These can really only be obtained by an adequately costed RCT. (For a much better account of RCTs the reader is referred to P. D. Oldham's book *Measurement in Medicine*, published by English Universities Press, London, 1968.)

5

Effectiveness and efficiency

Some aspects of preventive medicine under the NHS are so effective, both absolutely and in comparison with therapeutic medicine, that it seems a good idea to start with it in order to set the standard, and it seems right to start with the immunization programme which is the most effective part of preventive medicine.

It is true that some elements in the programme such as immunization for diphtheria are not supported by RCTs. The introduction of vaccine preceded the use of RCTs but there is a wealth of observational evidence to support its effectiveness. The rest of the programme has been based entirely on RCTs—both the introduction of new vaccines and the improvement of old ones. It is an example to the whole of medicine.

Some criticisms have reasonably been made. Dr Springett and I once suggested (5) that BCG might be abandoned when it costs more to prevent a case of tuberculosis through BCG vaccination than to treat a new case of TB when it occurred. We were then comparing BCG with other preventive measures. If one compares BCG on a cost/benefit basis with large sections of therapeutic medicine, BCG seems such a good bargain that it might seem wrong to abandon the former before the latter. However, if there are two ways, both equally effective, the overall working of the NHS would be improved by using the cheaper, whatever is going on in other spheres.

From an efficiency point of view even the immunization programme does not appear perfect; for example, the use of computers in West Sussex has apparently increased the coverage of these programmes at reduced cost (6, 7). This seems an example which should be followed.

Apart from the immunization programme the record of the NHS is patchy. There are sins of omission and commission. Of the latter the introduction of the programme of cervical smears in the hope of preventing carcinoma of the cervix is the saddest. It illustrates so clearly the consequences of assuming a hypothesis is correct, and translating the consequences into routine clinical practice before testing it by an RCT. Scientifically the story is relatively simple. The original idea was undoubtedly a good one. It was taken up by enthusiasts and became rapidly almost a routine clinical practice in the USA. It soon spread to this country. When suggestions were earlier made of doing an RCT it was considered unethical and the same decision has been taken in all countries ever since. It is very difficult to test the hypothesis by observational evidence. The death-rate from carcinoma of the cervix was falling before smears were introduced and has continued to fall at roughly the same rate in most areas. No convincing evidence has been published of a greater fall of this death-rate in areas where there has been a high coverage of the female population when compared with similar areas where little such work has been done. The difficulty in interpreting any difference in rates of fall of death-rates from carcinoma of the cervix (if it ever occurs) will be considerable. Areas in which there is a high coverage with smears nearly always have a much increased incidence of hysterectomy and (as would be expected) a higher percentage of invasive carcinoma diagnosed at an earlier stage. If this later alters the natural history of disease it will be almost impossible to decide which of these three factors is causing the difference.

It appears to me still possible that smears may have some preventive effect, but we may never know, and the health services of the world may well expend thousands of millions of pounds in the hope of preventing a relatively rare though severe condition whose mortality rate is decreasing fairly rapidly.

Sad too was the behaviour of journalists and television interviewers (as well as many doctors) when the subject was being debated in the UK. Never has there been less appeal to evidence and more to opinion. The Sunday papers and the weeklies took the subject up and I remember particularly a television programme which 'sold' cervical smears in a frighteningly effective way. I also remember giving a lecture in Cardiff on 'Screening' in 1967 into which I introduced the (as I thought) innocuous phrase 'I know of no hard evidence, at present, that cervical smears are effective.' To my surprise I was pilloried in the local Welsh press, who quoted many anonymous colleagues who thought me a 'dangerous heretic' and I received many abusive letters, some from colleagues. One very distinguished colleague wrote (rather irrelevantly) accusing me of 'causing misery to thousands by telling lay people that there was no cure for carcinoma of the cervix'. I wrote and asked him what his evidence was that carcinoma of the cervix could be cured but he did not answer. It was a pity as I have always wanted to know.

Having been long-winded on one sin of commission, I will be brief in my comments on sins of omission. The two most obvious are the prevention of cigarette smoking and population control. The former has been dealt with so adequately by the report of the Royal College of Physicians (8) that I have nothing to add except to link it to the second sin. We would, I think, be well advised, before encouraging everyone to give up smoking cigarettes, to control our population increase.

To me it is entirely obvious that the world in general and the inhabited part of the UK in particular is already overcrowded, but I admit this is a value judgement. There is no way of proving it; I would, however, like to make a few points. Some day, if we continue at our present rate of increase, a majority of the population will wake up and decide the country is overpopulated and demand action. It will then, of course, be much too late. It seems not unreasonable to try out a few possibilities now such as birth control and abortion. A high percentage of pregnancies appear to be unwanted, so it seems unreasonable in our present permissive society to force a woman to have a baby she does not want. It would be hard, I agree, on my gynaecological colleagues because I can appreciate the fact that the operation of abortion is often unpleasant and that some of the clients do not appear as particularly worthy citizens, but abortions are less demanding on the resources of the NHS than childbirth and it is surely up to the gynaecologists to do the necessary research to make abortion a brief safe event in out-patient departments. I put abortion first because I doubt if making the contraceptive pill or other methods easier to obtain and encouraging vasectomies will really have the desired effect.

Yet another reason is the simple fact that there is no way in which the quality of our lives could be improved by increasing our population, and if this is insufficient possibly some may be moved by the argument that the world is overcrowded in relation to its resources and that it is the UK's duty to set an example to the world.

This is undoubtedly by far the greatest sin of omission with which the Department is associated. Overpopulation could easily be described as the country's greatest problem, but it is, unfortunately, difficult to persuade people about it. I have only one practical suggestion to make. For the moment I think it would be of great assistance if ' refusal to abort ' was registered confidentially in the same way as ' abortion '.

2. TREATMENT

If anyone had any doubts about the need for doing RCTs to evaluate therapy, recent publications using this technique have given ample warning of how dangerous it is to assume that well-established therapies which have not been tested are always effective. Possibly the most striking result is Dr Mather's RCT in Bristol (9) in which hospital treatment (including a variable time in a coronary care unit) was compared with treatment at home for acute ischaemic heart disease. The results (which are discussed elsewhere, p. 51) do not suggest that there is any medical gain in admission to hospital with coronary care units compared with treatment at home. Equally striking are the results of the multi-centre American trial on the value of oral anti-diabetic therapy, insulin, and diet in the treatment of mature diabetics which are also discussed elsewhere (p. 54) (10, 11). They suggest that giving tolbutamide and phenformin is definitely disadvantageous, and that there is no advantage in giving insulin compared with diet. Dr Elwood, in my unit, has demonstrated very beautifully how ill-founded was the general view of the value of iron in non-pregnant women with haemoglobin levels between 9 g and 12 g per 100 ml in curing the classical symptoms of anaemia (12), while Dr Waters, also of my unit, has undermined the widespread belief in the value of ergotamine tartrate in the treatment of newly diagnosed cases of migraine (13).

I have neither the ability, knowledge, time, or space to classify all present-day therapies. All I feel capable of is a rough classification:

1. Those therapies, with no backing from RCTs, which are justified by their immediate and obvious effect, for example, insulin for acute juvenile diabetes, vitamin B_{12} for pernicious anaemia, penicillin for certain infections, etc.

2. Those therapies backed by RCTs. The best example is the drug therapy of tuberculosis, but there are, of course, many others.

3. Those where there is good experimental evidence of some effect, haematological, biochemical, physiological, or psychological, but no evidence from RCTs, of doing more good than harm to the patient, particularly in the long term. This is a very interesting and important group, because medical people are too easily bemused by evidence from what appears to be a more basic science. A good example, mentioned above, is the effect of iron on raising haemoglobin levels. This rise is very simply demonstrated, and there was a general belief that raising the haemoglobin level cured all the symptoms traditionally associated with low levels, until Dr Elwood published his results. The popular tranquillizers, antidepressants, and other psychometric drugs are also in this group. The vast majority of these drugs have been shown to have some psychometric effect, but the problem of whether in the long term they do more good than harm is unresolved.

4. Those therapies which were well established before the advent of RCTs whose effectiveness cannot be assessed because of the ethical situation, but where there is some real doubt about the effectiveness, for example treatment for carcinoma of the bronchus and of the breast (14).

5. Those therapies where the evidence from RCTs is equivocal. The best example (which is discussed later, p. 60) is tonsillectomy.

6. Those therapies under-investigated by RCT, although there are no ethical constraints, which are over-ripe for them. Psychotherapy and physiotherapy are probably the most important members of this group.

Effectiveness and efficiency

It would obviously be useful and important to divide the present NHS therapy proportionally into these groups, but there is really insufficient data to do so.

If effectiveness has been rather under-investigated, efficiency has hardly been investigated at all. I have already explained the extent of the meaning I have attached to the word in relation to the diagnosis and treatment of a particular disease. It can clearly be used to describe actions at other than a clinical level, for example, regional board and department level, but I believe that the correctness of the decisions taken at higher levels are so dependent on accurate information about the effectiveness and efficiency of the treatment of individual diseases that I want to concentrate the discussion at that level by attempting a classification of the various types of inefficiency.

1. The most important type of inefficiency is really a combination of two separate groups, the use of ineffective therapies and the use of effective therapies at the wrong time. They are closely connected; for instance I should, without thinking, have classified tonics as ineffective but many of them contain medicaments which could be effective in some circumstances. Iron and the vitamins, which are common ingredients of tonics, can, of course, on occasions be very effective. It is important to distinguish the very respectable, conscious use of placebos. The effect of placebos has been shown by RCTs to be very large. Their use in the correct place is to be encouraged. What is inefficient is the use of relatively expensive drugs as placebos. It is a pity some enterprising drug company does not produce a wide range of cheap, brightly coloured, non-toxic placebos. The main body of this group consist of cough mixtures, tonics, and haematinics. We do not know exactly how important they are as we have no national data connecting diagnosis and treatment and it is difficult to classify prescriptions as inefficient without this knowledge, but the amount of inefficient prescribing is undoubtedly very large, and from the point of view of the NHS very expensive. The millions of pounds spent by the NHS on vitamins is evidence enough. One other type of inefficiency deserves a mention; the use of effective therapies routinely in relation to specific diagnoses when the

31

evidence of effectiveness is negligible or nonexistent in these particular cases, for example vitamin B_{12} for herpes zoster and multiple sclerosis (15).

At the other end of the scale are the therapies for which there is no evidence of effectiveness, but where something has to be done. Simple mastectomy is a case in point for carcinoma of the breast. This I do not consider inefficient, but on present evidence I would not classify the use of radical mastectomy as efficient (14).

2. The incorrect place of treatment. This is possibly the least-recognized type of inefficiency, but it seems probable that the increasing cost of hospitalization will force attention to it. There are in general five places where treatment can be given: at the GP's surgery, at home, at the out-patient department, in hospital, or more recently in a 'community' hospital (see p. 34). Traditions have grown up as to the correct place for treatment for particular diseases, and until very recently no one has treated these traditional decisions as hypotheses which should be tested. I have already mentioned Dr Mather's comparison of the treatment of acute ischaemic heart disease at home and in a hospital with a coronary care unit. Farquharson in 1955 demonstrated the possibility of performing operations for hernia in the out-patient department but did not have an adequate control group (16). Weddell has compared the treatment of varicose veins in hospital and in the out-patient department using the RCT technique (17). No evidence was found of any advantage associated with hospitalization for those cases without skin damage. A comparison between the care of patients with a chronic disease through regular out-patient visits and that under GP care is now planned. It is to be hoped that such demonstrations that RCTs are possible and ethical will encourage others to follow suit in this new sphere.

3. Incorrect length of stay in hospital. It is not surprising, given the economic and psychological facts of the NHS, that the average length of stay in hospital in this country is higher than in some other countries. Professor Logan and his associates have performed a great service in calling attention to these figures (18). In addition, evidence has been accumulating of large differences in length of stay between regions and between different consultants

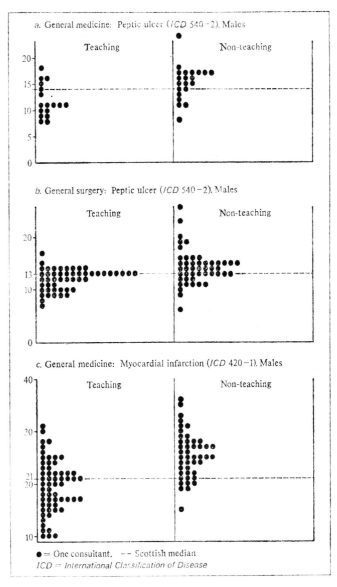

a. General medicine: Peptic ulcer (*ICD* 540-2). Males

b. General surgery: Peptic ulcer (*ICD* 540-2). Males

c. General medicine: Myocardial infarction (*ICD* 420-1). Males

● = One consultant. -- Scottish median
ICD = *International Classification of Disease*

FIGURE 5.1. Median duration of stay in days for two diagnoses for individual consultants in Scotland (data for 1967)

when treating the same disease. The most striking evidence (and the most accurate) comes from Heasman and Carstairs (19) from whose paper Figure 5.1 is taken. The extent of the differences is really surprising when hospitalization in a district general hospital is one of the costliest treatments that can be prescribed, and that the majority of patients wish to leave hospital as soon as possible. The only condition in which length of stay has been much investigated is again hernia. Blodgett and Beattie (20) were first to publish a controlled series. One group were discharged on the first day post-operatively. Morris, Ward, and Handyside (21) have also reported a similar controlled series. In neither were any serious disadvantages of early discharge noted, but early discharge of herniorraphies has hardly become routine. The mean length of stay for hernia in England and Wales in 1967 was 9·1 days for males.

Unfortunately this observational evidence does not take us very far. All the consultants cannot be right, but this does not help us to determine the optimum length of stay. This can again be best approached by RCTs, but it will not be easy. The main index will have to be the incidence of complications and as these will in general not be high, very large populations are required to establish an optimum.

At this stage I want to interpolate a short discussion about the so-called 'community' hospitals (22), as they are very relevant to the last two points about inefficiency. The cottage hospital is the direct ancestor of the community hospital and I was brought up in a town, Galashiels, which had such a cottage hospital. I have clearcut memories of that hospital, which fully support the two main points at present being made in favour of community hospitals. Everyone now knows the problems associated with visiting hospital patients but when visiting friends in the cottage hospital in Galashiels I was able to visit on foot. There is no doubt that a community hospital would be easier to visit than a district general hospital. The other point is local pride. Every community which is a sociological entity needs foci of interest and the cottage hospital certainly was one such focus which made it the recipient of voluntary help and financial aid in a way a district general hospital serving largely ill-defined areas can never hope to emulate

The NHS would be unwise to neglect this. The defects of the old cottage hospitals are well known. They attempted too much and finally became dangerous. If, however, I understand the modern concept of a community hospital correctly, only those patients would be admitted for whom hard evidence existed that there was little risk of medical detriment in treating them in the community hospital as opposed to the district general hospital. If this is so, such community hospitals would be of great value in reducing the last two types of inefficiency. For instance if an RCT showed that a certain disease could be treated as successfully at home as in hospital there would always be a certain number of people who for social reasons could not be treated at home. A community hospital would be ideal for them. In order for all patients to be discharged at the optimum time, community hospitals would serve two purposes, to take those who for social reasons could not go straight home after the optimum time but could go to a community hospital, and those who are kept in hospital only for observation which can be carried out as efficiently in the community hospital.

I am conscious that I have only scratched the surface of inefficiency. I could have stressed the rising percentage of hospital admissions for iatrogenic diseases; I could have stirred the dirty waters of medical administration, but I think for my limited purposes I have done enough.

3. DIAGNOSIS

I have, rather illogically, put diagnosis last of this trio. One would expect it to come first or at least second. I consider much less thinking has gone into the theory underlying diagnosis, or possibly one should say less energy has gone into constructing the correct model of diagnostic procedures, than into therapy or prevention where the concept of 'altering the natural history of the disease' has been generally accepted and a technique has been evolved for testing hypotheses concerning this. With diagnosis things are different. For one thing it grew up in advance of therapy. For a considerable period able clinicians had little else to do but refine the art of diagnosis. It became in this way almost disassociated from treatment and became regarded, consciously or unconsciously, as an end in itself. In conversation, but not in writing, it is still possible to find intelligent clinicians who would argue that the general objective of diagnosis was to describe the patient as completely as possible in medico-scientific terms. If this is the real objective it becomes almost impossible to apply the idea of effectiveness and the economics of diagnosis would merely be a blank cheque to the laboratory and clinicians.

As regards the mechanics of diagnosis, the best description is by Medawar (23). He uses diagnosis as an example of the rapid, almost unconscious, use of the hypothetico-deductive system, which is generally accepted as *the* scientific system. He sees the doctor, as he takes the history and examines the patient, as considering a whole series of hypotheses, suggested by the signs and symptoms and rejected or confirmed by further signs and symptoms. He does not discuss the use of further tests, but I am entirely convinced that his description is basically correct, if rather flattering. I imagine, however, he would agree that some clinicians are more 'hypothetico-deductive' than others. This unfortunately does not help us about the objectives that must be defined before discussing effectiveness.

To solve the problem the best approach is to look for the simplest possible diagnostic situation, and this is undoubtedly screening where one diagnostic test is applied to large populations. Screening became increasingly popular in the late 1950s, largely on the assumption that the discovery of any abnormality was worthwhile. Fortunately the underlying theory came up for considerable discussion and in course of time a more rational suggestion emerged. This, in brief, was that a test was suitable as a diagnostic screening test if there was hard evidence, preferably based on RCTs, that the application of the test to populations, followed by suitable therapy where needed, would alter the natural history of the disease in an appreciable proportion of the cases screened at a reasonable cost (24). This approach makes a very big difference to the practice of screening. Relatively few screening procedures come up to these standards. Can this approach be applied to diagnosis as a whole? It is only fair to point out that there is a difference between screening and clinical diagnosis. The 'screener' is in an evangelical situation. His cry is 'Come unto me, ye faithful, and I will cure your piles.' He is definitely advertising and promising a result. In the clinical situation the patient seeks the doctor and it is the doctor's duty to do his best. I personally think the same approach that has been used for screening can be applied to clinical diagnosis, although some modifications are necessary because of the increased complexity of the clinical situation. For instance, if an acceptable screening test for a particular disease is applied to a population there are two outcomes. In a small minority a certain disease in which there is evidence that treatment is effective is diagnosed, and in the vast majority it is excluded: at a reasonable level of probability. The same test diagnoses and excludes. In the clinical situation the objectives are more complex. The main objective, as in screening, is to diagnose a treatable disease, but in addition there are other objectives such as diagnosing other treatable diseases and excluding them. In addition there are certain limited social advantages in diagnosing untreatable disease. If this is accepted we clearly need the value of the tests involved in the complex diagnostic process to be weighted in such a way that due priority is given to the diagnosis of 'treatable' disease but lesser weight to exclusion of treatable disease and the diagnosis of incurable disease. This, of course, would mean a radical reorientation in the methods of evaluating diagnostic tests. At present the main arguments in favour of particular tests are the high yield of abnormals, the high correlation with pathology at post-mortem or operation, and the increased understanding of the case given to the doctor by the test results. It is of interest that the welfare of the patient figures so little in these methods of evaluation: though there is, I must admit, some hope for him at second hand.

I feel the only hope for the development of effective diagnostic procedures in the future is for the discipline proposed for screening to be adopted with the necessary modifications. It will be difficult to work out the necessary weightings, but I understand that Professor Card in Glasgow is hard at work on this. In the meantime there is a great deal that can be done by crude RCTs. I can imagine some fascinating results emerging from randomizing pulmonary function tests in chest out-patients, tomograms and lateral and oblique radiographs in sputum positive cases of tuberculosis, barium meals in gastric out-patients, and X-rays of the back for back-ache in general practice. I wonder if there would be any significant differences in the natural history of the two groups?

Turning now to efficiency I want first to discuss reproducibility. Signs and symptoms have been with us for a long time, but relatively little has been done to standardize and render reproducible these 'bits' of information. The measurement of medical observer error became fashionable in the early 1950s and a certain amount was done to standardize the methods of eliciting signs and symptoms and measuring their reproducibility. Much good work was done leading to standardized reproducible questionnaires which have been validated in various ways for respiratory and cardiovascular symptoms (25, 26). Mental symptoms too have been investigated, but there remain large unexplored areas. Physical signs have attracted even less attention after a promising beginning (27), and there are even bigger fields requiring attention, in order to make the bits of information as useful as possible.

As regards laboratory tests I have always found it surprising how uninterested clinicians are in the 'between, and within, laboratory variation' in test results. Epidemiologists, making measurements on defined communities, often use the same laboratory facilities as the clinician and the preliminary investigations of the reproducibility of laboratory work made by the epidemiologists often alarm them so much that they go elsewhere or do the work themselves. One particular facet which worried me personally about laboratory biochemical work is the almost complete lack of interest in whether the blood was taken fasting, the time interval and temperature of the blood between taking and spinning, and spinning and analysis. It is, I suppose, reasonable for clinicians not to be as obsessional as epidemiologists, and that they should not be so interested in 'between laboratory' variation, but I am surprised they have not insisted much more on the reduction of 'within laboratory' variation. One can only conclude that the results are not particularly important in clinical decision-making. There were great hopes that automation would solve all the problems of reproducibility, but the first published results for haematology are very depressing indeed (28). They may improve.

Most of the remarks so far apply to haematological and bio-chemical tests rather than radiological. These latter are in rather a special position because of the associated risks. Much had un-doubtedly been done in reducing the dosage received by the patient for a particular investigation, but the number of tests continue to increase rapidly. There has also probably been a general improvement in radiographic technique, which was vital to improvements in safety and reproducibility. The interpretation of chest radiographs was the subject of the original investigation which led to the widespread interest in medical observer error and this undoubtedly had some general effect on radiology, but there is still a tendency for new techniques to get into general circulation before being properly tested. For instance Elwood and Pitman (29), in a study of the differences between eight radiologists in the detection of Paterson–Kelly webs in photographs of the barium swallow X-ray films of 132 subjects with dysphagia, found the number of subjects in whom a web was detected varied from 6 per cent to 59 per cent.

The interpretation of test results is the next point I want to take up. Some results are easy to interpret, particularly when the answers are couched in terms of 'positive' and 'negative' or 'present' and 'absent', but the majority of tests particularly haema-tological and biochemical ones now produce quantitative answers which are harder to interpret. The evolution of this problem is summarized in Figure 5.2. I was originally given the impression as a student that the diagnostic characteristics of ill and healthy people were widely different. I suppose this idea remained un-consciously with me until my colleagues and myself started examining the populations of the Rhondda Fach and the Vale of Glamorgan. Dr Miall's measurement of the distribution of arterial blood pressures of a random sample of the population was probably the one that educated me most (30). The great Sir Thomas Lewis had taught me that those with diastolic pressures above 100 mmHg were 'hypertensive'. I certainly expected the distribution to be bimodal as in the second line of the diagram, but instead we found the slightly skewed distribution seen on the bottom line. Some will remember the long and interesting battle in the medical press between the 'Pickeringites' and the

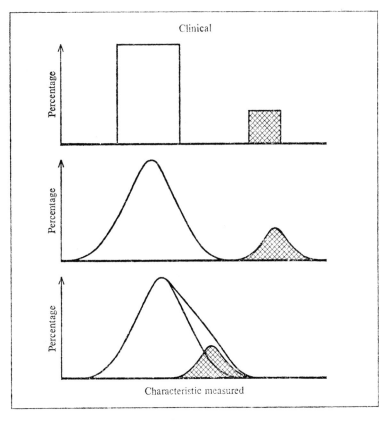

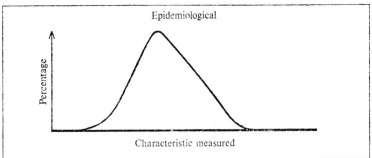

FIGURE 5.2. Clinical and epidemiological interpretations of distributions of quantitative biological characteristics

'Plattites' ending, in my opinion, in an overwhelming victory for the Pickeringites. Since then my colleagues and I have measured the distribution on random samples of defined populations of many physiological and biochemical variates. We have never found a true bimodal distribution, though, of course, the degree of skewness varies considerably. The few reports of bi- or multimodality have always been explicable on the basis of digit preference, observer bias, or population selection. Possibly the most extreme case from my point of view was the examination of 152 out of 153 of the living descendants of my great grandfather about whom there was considerable evidence that he suffered from porphyria variegata (31). This is inherited as a dominant gene and there was every reason to expect a bimodal distribution, but in fact the actual distribution is only severely skewed (Figure 5.3). (An alternative hypothesis is, of course, that I was examining the descendants of the wrong great grandfather.)

Once the idea of a skewed distribution became partially accepted, there was considerable pressure, conscious and unconscious, to provide the physicians with a simple rule to tell them what it all meant and someone (I have been unable to discover who it was) introduced the concept of 'normal limits' and defined them as lying within plus or minus two standard deviations from the mean. Theoretically there is nothing to support this idea. It is merely the statement of an assumption that 5 per cent of the population when described quantitatively by any test are abnormal. It also assumes that deviations from the mean in either direction are equally important and that doctors should take action if the results fall outside these limits, to say nothing of assuming that standard deviations are meaningful when calculated on very skew distributions, and the very oddly selected populations on which the calculations are based.

The only alternative to this unsatisfactory approach, as far as I know, is that suggested by Dr Elwood and myself. The idea is that for simple univariate analyses the object should be to establish the point or points on the distribution at which therapy begins to do more good than harm. Elwood has demonstrated the application of this approach in his investigation of the distribution of haemoglobin levels in the population as an indication for giving

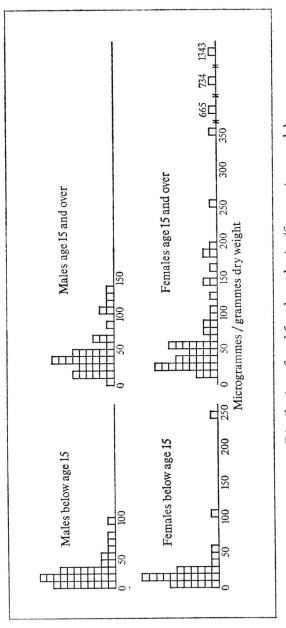

FIGURE 5.3. Distribution of total faecal porphyrins (first specimens only)

iron therapy (32). Similar approaches have been used by Keen in relation to blood sugar levels (33), Graham in relation to intra-ocular pressure (34), and by others in relation to arterial blood pressure (35, 36, 37) although those on blood pressure have been carried out on somewhat selected populations. It is very sobering to reflect how few distributions have been investigated at all in this way.

A less important, but interesting, problem is the order in which tests should be done. I was brought up in an older tradition. I was told 'Before ordering a test decide what you will do if it is (*a*) positive, or (*b*) negative, and if both answers are the same don't do the test.' At the other end of the scale is the most recent innovation whereby a package of results of a dozen tests arrive at the bedside almost before the signs and symptoms have been elicited. The former approach is logically unassailable, but can be criticized on the grounds of delay. The same criticism cannot be levelled at the latter, but the only trial of the value of this package was not very reassuring. This was an RCT to see whether it reduced length of stay in hospital (38). The variable results may, of course, have been due to the consultants' lack of understanding of the meaning of all the measurements.

One sophisticated approach to multiple testing is the Wayne (or Newcastle) scale (39) in the diagnosis of thyrotoxicosis. In this the correct weighting for a series of symptoms has been worked out to help clinicians decide, with a small error, whether more complex and expensive tests are necessary. This, I think, gives us a lead towards a possible solution to the general problem. Computers will be invaluable in this work but at present such work is directed towards correlations with pathology and not towards the outcome from the patients' point of view.

I do not intend to go into any great detail about the risks associated with tests. These have been published in relation to particular tests, but they are usually from very selected series. A definitive study of the risk of tests in relation to mortality and morbidity is badly needed. Similarly with costs; we have not yet got a satisfactory costing system which would enable the costs of tests in every hospital to be compared. We badly need a list of costs in large letters in every out-patient, ward, and GP consulting room.

One other point is worth making about the efficiency of diagnostic tests from a different angle. Considerable demands are made on laboratories by phenomenological research and 'pseudo-research' which is endemic in many hospitals, particularly in teaching hospitals. I have omitted here all discussion of laboratory organization for the good reason that I know very little about it, but it is clearly of great importance in efficiency.

With the ever-increasing demand for pathological and radio-logical investigations something must be done to introduce some measure of effectiveness and some control of efficiency. The suggestions made here may not be perfect but I believe they are on the right lines.

6

Illustrative examples

I. PULMONARY TUBERCULOSIS

The change in the tuberculosis world between 1944 when I was burying my POW tuberculous patients in Germany and the present day when TB deaths are the subject of a special investigation, as in theory they should not happen, is one of the most cheering things I have experienced in my life. The way in which the new treatments and preventive measures were introduced can also serve as a model for the introduction of all new treatments in the future. RCTs were used from the very beginning, and through this the correct dosages and combination of drugs were quickly established; 'resistance to drugs' was quickly identified and means found of preventing it; each new drug was carefully assessed as it came on the market. The sad story of BCG was finally ended by the Medical Research Council's RCT. The result is that there now are effective methods of treatment and prevention for TB. The speed of its development is very much to the credit of the MRC, WHO, and the British Tuberculosis Association, but it would have been impossible without the technique of the RCT.

On the efficiency side there is also a great deal to the credit of this branch of medicine. 'Place of treatment' was first investigated by an RCT when hospital and home care for the tuberculous were compared in Madras (40) and various studies in this country and the USA have confirmed the Madras finding that bed rest was unimportant (41, 42, 43). In addition there were two excellent studies showing 100 per cent conversion from sputum 'positive' to sputum 'negative' in Birmingham and Edinburgh for all patients diagnosed during one year (44, 45).

It really looks at first as if this were an example of an effective therapy efficiently applied. Unfortunately if one looks a little more closely the general situation, although very good, is not perfect.

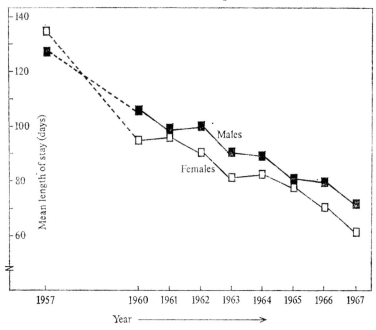

FIGURE 6.1. Mean length of hospital stay (days) for patients with respiratory tuberculosis (*ICD*, 7th revision, causes 001–008) in England and Wales, 1957–67

In spite of the striking evidence about the unimportance of bed rest, it is surprising to find how slowly the mean length of stay in hospitals in England and Wales is falling (Figure 6.1), and how much the variation in length of stay seems to depend on individual consultants (Figure 6.2). The unsatisfactory results that can be obtained by the usual type of treatment in England and Wales (hospitalization for three months with triple therapy until the report on drug 'sensitivity' was available, followed by two drugs on an out-patient basis for eighteen months) is well illustrated by the report on the Gateshead follow-up (46). The real problem is how to ensure that patients take their chemotherapy after leaving hospital. Some doctors react by keeping their patients longer in

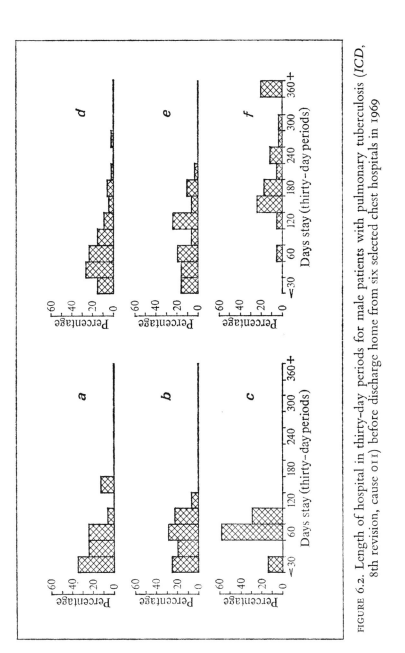

FIGURE 6.2. Length of hospital in thirty-day periods for male patients with pulmonary tuberculosis (*ICD*, 8th revision, cause 011) before discharge home from six selected chest hospitals in 1969

hospital, others, as in Gateshead, try biweekly supervised chemo-therapy. The correct solution is still unknown, and until it is the treatment will not be completely efficient.

There are other details which need tidying up. There are remarkable differences for instance in radiographic routine. In an unpublished study of a twelve-month follow-up of all cases admitted during one year (47) the type of case admitted to three hospitals were reasonably comparable, but in one hospital only 10 per cent, in another 52 per cent, and in the third 85 per cent had at least one tomogram. Similar differences were found in the use of lateral radiographs, and in the frequency of sputum testing. There is a tendency to concentrate sputum tests in the first fews months after beginning therapy and to use radiographs rather than sputum tests to monitor the course of the disease. It is, I agree, often difficult to obtain sputum, but sputum results are very much more valuable.

Some one, rather sardonically, asked me once how far I was 'prepared to take this randomizing game'. I answered, without thinking, 'You should randomize until it hurts (the clinicians).' In spite of my great admiration for the effective therapy and the efficiency with which it has been applied in this field I still think there is room for improvement. The TB world has not random-ized until it hurts.

2. ARTERIAL BLOOD PRESSURE

Specific hypotensive treatment for hypertension started shortly after the discovery of anti-tuberculous therapy, but the subsequent history therapeutically has been very different. In the tuberculosis world there were about a hundred RCTs, while in the blood pressure world there have been very few. The reasons for this are not immediately obvious. It was not due to lack of research interest in the problems of blood pressure, nor was it due to a lack of intelligent people working in the field. In both, arterial pressure was probably better served than TB. The system of notification and the existence of sanatoria were of great help in organizing RCTs of anti-tuberculous therapies but probably the critical factor was the tradition of 'pure' research which has always considered

RCTs a rather borderline activity, and the arterial pressure research world has always been on the 'purish' side.

Once effective methods of treatment were discovered the scope of treatment was clear. All the epidemiological evidence has supported the idea that elevation of the diastolic pressure above 90 mmHg or a corresponding elevation of systolic pressure is highly correlated with a decreased expectation of life (48). This correlation is all the more impressive because it is based on a 'casual' measurement of arterial pressure which has a considerable inter- and intra-observer difference. It does not necessarily follow from these observations that lowering arterial pressure will prolong life, but it strongly encourages the research worker to use RCTs to test the hypothesis. The few RCTs (35, 36, 37) that have been carried out so far have fully confirmed that life can be prolonged by lowering the pressure. Briefly the results so far apply to men between the ages of 45 and 70, whose symptoms were sufficiently severe to take them to hospital and whose diastolic pressure was above about 100 mmHg. There is no evidence relevant to women. There is, in addition, reasonable observational evidence that the hypotensive drugs are very effective in the treatment of malignant hypertension in men and women. It is generally agreed that it would be unethical to randomize anyone of either sex with a diastolic pressure of 120 mmHg or more. The gaps in our knowledge are therefore related to women and to asymptomatic men with diastolic pressures less than 120 mmHg. (Systolic pressure has equal prognostic value, but diastolic pressure is more customary in the literature.)

The question therefore arises as to the use made of this limited research input by the NHS and it is encouraging to note that there has been a considerable fall in the SMR for hypertensive diseases (*ICD*, 7th revision, 440–3). Taking the SMR in 1950–2 as 100 for both sexes the SMR in 1967 was 40 for males and 45 for females. On the other hand there has been no decrease in the ' certified time lost' through hypertensive disease. It does appear that this is an example of an effective therapy which has been only partially efficiently applied, partly because not all those for whom treatment is indicated by present evidence are being treated but also, more importantly, because of the lack of knowledge about the effectiveness of treatment in some age/sex symptomatic groups.

Before blaming the research world for this situation, it is only fair to point out how very difficult such research is. The size of the populations required is frightening. For instance, to measure the value of hypertensive therapy in unselected cases with diastolic pressures between 95 and 109 mmHg in men aged 35–44 using a two-tailed test and expecting a reduction of 30 per cent in the morbid events in the ten-year follow-up in the cases as compared with the controls, a population of about 18,000 cases and 18,000 controls would be needed. This is calculated on the basis of a 95 per cent chance of obtaining a difference that is statistically significant at the 5 per cent level. (The numbers would be very much smaller if there was evidence that ischaemic heart disease cases would be prevented.) In addition, the problem of 'drop-outs' would add about 20 per cent to the number required. Above all there is the tremendous problem of finding suitable cases. The prevalence of this range of pressure in the general population in this age/sex group is about 25 per cent, so about 100,000 and 70,000 people would have to be screened. The problem of keeping asymptomatic people on treatment for ten years is also a serious one, so the future is scarcely promising.

3. ISCHAEMIC HEART DISEASE

Ischaemic heart disease (IHD) presents a different type of problem for evaluation from my particular point of view. Since its recognition as a clinical entity in the 1930s, rest has been the main therapy and it is sad to say that even now we have no idea how much rest is indicated for any particular case. Several specific therapies have been suggested and introduced without preliminary trials, but the trials have followed rapidly. The best-known example is 'anti-coagulant therapy'. This treatment has been subjected to a large number of RCTs, but the value of such therapy is still in doubt. It seems probable that the treatment gives no striking over-all benefit, but may be of value in certain subgroups. These subgroups, however, are not present in sufficiently large numbers in the individual trials to warrant definite conclusions. An attempt to get around this difficulty by pooling the data from the best trials by an international anticoagulant review group (49) led to the conclusion that there was no benefit for women and that the benefit for men was restricted to those with prolonged angina and/or previous infarction. The group suggested that further trials on these two subgroups were necessary.

'Insulin, glucose and potassium' had a shorter period of glory. It was ushered in with the usual statement by a member of the medical establishment that the evidence was so good that an RCT would be unethical, but much to everyone's credit the RCT was carried out (50) and the treatment has now practically disappeared. Both these examples underline on the one hand the need for meticulously planned RCTs on large numbers and on the other hand for more than one such trial to be carried out, particularly if the numbers are relatively small and the 5 per cent level of significance is used.

The battle for the 'coronary care units' is just beginning. The coronary care unit (CCU) is basically an American product. Modern technology made it simple to monitor patients' hearts and the evidence that a defibrillator could deal with a large proportion of cardiac arrests was easily established. The combination in a coronary care unit was irresistible in the USA and it was only our relative poverty and the existence of an NHS which aimed at equality that prevented it sweeping the UK.

In support of the CCU a considerable amount of observational data was produced, mainly comparing case-fatality rates before and after the introduction of CCUs. There was little or no evidence that the groups were comparable but it looked as though the CCUs would win the day by default. It was therefore much to the credit of Mather and his colleagues (and to Lord Platt who chaired the committee which recommended the trial) that they suggested and carried through a trial comparing the treatment of IHD at home and in hospital with a CCU (9). This was technically and psychologically very difficult indeed. Their results are still being debated, but it seems worth while making a few points:

1. I believe that randomization was achieved between the 'randomized-home' and 'randomized-hospital' groups. The criticism that it was impossible to randomize the complete

population of IHDs in the area is a poor one as it applies to nearly all RCTs ever carried out. It is very much to their credit that they collected so much information about those who were not randomized.

2. This trial does not suggest that all CCUs are useless. In the first place the trial should be repeated in another area. In the second it tells us nothing about those cases which have to be admitted to hospital with IHD because they cannot, for social reasons, be treated at home, nor about those who have an attack while in hospital. In both cases, on the present evidence, it would seem reasonable to continue using CCUs.

3. The simplest hypothesis to explain the results is that some people become so frightened by removal from home into CCUs (and/or hospitals) that cardiac arrest is more frequent than when they are at home. The first part of the hypothesis is certainly supported by most of what I have seen in CCUs in the USA and the UK in comparison with the patients I have seen at home, but my experience is inevitably highly selected.

4. The future is difficult to guess. The CCU (and hospital) may become less frightening—either by internal change or by alteration in patients' attitude. The CCU may develop new technological tricks which counterbalance the advantages of home treatment. On the other hand anti-arrythmic drugs may be developed which improve home therapy. The great point is that, after Mather and his colleagues, all these innovations will, I am sure, be carefully monitored by RCTs.

5. It would be wrong to leave this subject without calling attention to the fact that Dr Mather's trial is the first major trial financed by the new Research Section of the Department of Health and Social Security. It augurs well for the future.

The other relevant trial is that by Hofvendahl (51). In this the two treatments were not randomly allocated but he appears to have achieved reasonable comparability between the two groups. The results suggest that those treated for about forty-eight hours in a CCU have a significantly lower mortality than those treated in the same hospital, but in an ordinary ward. The simplest explanation of the findings in both trials is that admission to an ordinary ward has a deleterious effect compared with treatment at home, but that the deleterious effect can be partially reduced by a CCU. The very high mortality on the first day of the cases in the ordinary ward in Hofvendahl's series would support this.

It will clearly be very difficult to get a quick clearcut evaluation of CCUs. There is a great deal of bias, and a considerable amount of vested interest. The bias is beautifully illustrated by a story of the early days of Mather's trial. The first report after a few months of the trial showed a slightly greater death-rate in those treated in hospital than in those treated at home. Some one reversed the figures and showed them to a CCU enthusiast who immediately declared that the trial was unethical, and must be stopped at once. When, however, he was shown the table the correct way round he could not be persuaded to declare CCUs unethical!

As regards efficiency in IHD there are two major unsolved connected problems: 'length of stay in hospital' and 'time of complete bed rest'. The variation of length of stay in hospital for cases of IHD in Scotland is from ten to thirty-six days (19) and is probably similar in England and Wales. It seems possible that, even if it is confirmed that some types of IHD cases do better at home, some will have to be treated in hospital and it is urgent to know the optimum length of stay for uncomplicated cases. Even less is known about the time of complete bed rest before the patient is mobilized. It is believed to vary from two days to about thirty days. The urgency of discovering the optimum for this is even more obvious. It is cheering to hear that at least one RCT has been started to clarify this point.

So far, I have been discussing therapy after the doctor gets to the case. This is, on average, about four hours after the beginning of symptoms. By this time about 50 per cent of the deaths will have occurred, so, if the disease is to be brought under control therapeutically, some attempt has to be made to get to the cases earlier. Pantridge (52) pioneered the idea of 'coronary care ambulances' (CCA) in Belfast. This is an excellent idea, but it is difficult to evaluate and expensive in medical manpower. The best guess (and it is a guess) is that the effect is small. The task of estimating this reduction accurately by means of RCTs is a formidable one. It would probably require the co-operation of several cities, but on present evidence a CCA seems a better investment than a CCU.

The general picture is a gloomy one. The effective therapies (defibrillation and rest) appear to have been applied inefficiently. The cheering thing about the situation is that RCTs have been used in the past to measure the effect of therapies for this condition and are being used so at present. I have every confidence that their use will finally solve the problem, but I must again stress the enormous effort required to organize these sort of trials.

4. MATURE DIABETES

The evidence for the effect of therapy on death-rates in the case of diabetes as a whole has recently been reviewed by Reid and Evans (53). Following the discovery of insulin by Banting and Best there was a marked and continuing fall in the death-rate for both sexes between the ages of 15 and 44. The fall in death-rate under the age of 15 started somewhat later. It seems reasonable to associate these changes with the introduction of insulin. In the older age-groups the position is very different. The graph has undulated rather than fallen and in males is now rising fairly rapidly in all age-groups above the age of 35. There is therefore no clearcut evidence from death-rates of any effect of therapy on mature diabetes.

These mature diabetics are at present normally treated by diet and insulin or oral drugs such as tolbutamide and phenformin. The control of treatment is traditionally in a special hospital out-patient department. The basis for this therapy was that 'mature' diabetics had abnormally raised blood sugar curves, and it was assumed that drugs that were known to reduce the blood sugar would be beneficial. Until recently there was little experimental evidence. The results of two very well-designed trials are now available, but unfortunately they do not entirely agree. The most recent publications (10, 11) are from the UGDP group in the USA, whose results from a beautifully designed and executed multicentre trial clearly suggest from mortality data that tolbutamide and phenformin are dangerous and insulin without effect in these mature diabetics. The only serious criticism of this excellent trial is the lack of IHD deaths in the placebo group (Table I, p. 790 of the report) which is very much lower than world experience would suggest. It seems possible that, by bad luck, their randomization produced an atypical 'placebo' group in this respect.

The Guy's Hospital group in this country have completed an eight-year follow-up in Bedford of a very well-designed RCT (33) to compare the effect of diet and oral anti-diabetic therapy. Their patients differed considerably from those in the American trial in that the vast majority were found as a result of the preceding survey, while in the other the patients attended the clinics because of symptoms. They have found slightly fewer cardiovascular deaths in their tolbutamide group, but the difference did not reach conventional levels of significance. When, however, cardio-vascular 'events' are added to deaths in the two groups (tolbuta-mide and placebo) the difference does become significant at the 5 per cent level.

When two such well-designed trials differ in this way the only conclusion to be drawn is that tolbutamide has little or no effect. It may or may not be dangerous, but there seems little reason to risk using it. Similarly the American trial gives no evidence to support the use of insulin in these cases, though it is of course possible that future trials may show that certain drugs are effective in particular subgroups of mature diabetes.

The classical place of treatment of mature diabetes is an out-patient department and this seems open to considerable criticism. The original idea was a consultation where the patient was referred to a consultant for his opinion. The consultant examined the patient, wrote to the GP and the patient returned to his care. In the first quarter of this century the 'chronic' out-patient made his appearance. There were probably several causes for this:

1. Before we had an NHS many uninsured persons became chronic out-patients to avoid paying the GPs.

2. A desire for continuous surveillance of patients receiving, out-side hospital, effective but possibly dangerous therapy requiring special investigations and/or experience for its satisfactory control.

3. A desire to utilize such populations for research purposes.

4. Possibly some distrust on the part of the consultants of the abilities of the GPs and perhaps a desire for empire-building on the part of the consultants.

5. A lack by some GPs of time, interest in, or experience of, treating certain diseases. The desire by some family doctors to have certain diseases treated in hospital is understandable. If diabetes is taken as an example each doctor is only likely to have about ten to twenty diabetics in his practice and each of these may require a different therapeutic regime.

The idea of the chronic out-patient grew rapidly and there are, for instance, more than 3,000 diabetic out-patients in Cardiff alone. This growth has inevitably had serious consequences. Possibly the most serious is the disappearance of the idea of a 'consultation'. It is clearly impossible for each chronic out-patient to see a consultant every time he appears. Other consequences are the increased size of out-patient buildings and the increased staff required to run them; the increased ambulance services for the patients; the increased parking space round hospitals, the increased travelling for elderly ill patients, and the increased loss of time from work by otherwise fit patients.

At the same time the standards of general practice are rising. Health centres are being built and postgraduate medical education is spreading. There seems to be a very reasonable hope that some chronic out-patients could be looked after as well by the GP as in the out-patient department, thereby allowing more time and effort to be spent on those who do require hospital facilities. It is encouraging to hear that a trial is likely to be mounted soon to see if some chronic diabetic patients can be returned to the care of their GPs with advantage, or at any rate without medical detriment.

In general, the treatment of mature diabetics would seem to be an example of the large-scale use of ineffective and possibly dangerous therapies in a particularly inefficient way. The cause of the sad situation seems to be the assumption that if some bio-chemical parameter is abnormally distributed in a defined group of people, 'normalizing' the distribution must do more good than harm. In mature diabetes it may well be the wrong parameter that is being altered.

5. PSYCHIATRY

Many, I imagine, like myself thought in the mid 1950s that a great scientific renaissance in psychiatry was just round the corner. Everything seemed just right. The Freudians had produced some fascinating hypotheses, without bothering to test them. The biochemists were beginning to take an interest in mental disease and drug therapy was a real possibility. Psychology was appearing as an adequate supporting science. All the necessary techniques for RCTs, observer error studies, and community studies were worked out. There was a high standard of recruitment into psychiatric research and there was always Professor Eysenck in the wings to be the *Advocatus Diaboli*.

It would be very wrong to say that nothing has happened. A very great deal has changed in psychiatry but it does not add up to a scientific renaissance. The two big factors that have changed psychiatry have come from outside. There has been the marked change in social attitudes leading to the emergence of the permissive society which has affected nearly every aspect of our lives including attitudes towards mental abnormalities. There has also been a great increase in the discovery and marketing of psychotrophic drugs and psychiatry must be judged by the way it has used scientific methods to control the impact of these two factors on their patients and the public in order to achieve maximum benefit and minimum harm.

Both factors have probably helped to empty the mental hospitals into the community. This is mainly due to discharging schizophrenics. In the 1930s about 60 per cent of these stayed at least two years in hospital, now only 10 per cent stay as long. There seems reasonable evidence that phenothiazine improves the symptoms of schizophrenia in the short term, but there is much more doubt about its long-term effects, and when one looks for careful long-term controlled studies measuring not only the benefit to the patient but also the social burden on the family, and the general financial costs of care in the community compared with care in a modernized psychiatric hospital there is really no evidence at all. It seems to an outsider that the hostels and homes required for all the mental cases discharged into the community may be far more demanding on human and financial resources than anyone has envisaged.

The results of the introduction of the psychotrophic drugs has been dramatic. Prescriptions for barbiturates have now reached 20 million per annum; for phenothiazine tranquillizers, 6 million; amphetamine, 5 million; and non-barbiturate hypnotics, 5 million, etc. Such mass therapy could only be justified by clearcut results to clinical trials. There have, it is true, been many trials, some well designed and some not, but the most striking impression from the results of the well-designed ones is their variability. Leyburn (54) has summarized the contradictory results in an article which can be strongly recommended. It seems certain that there are unusual difficulties in carrying out RCTs in this area. Roth and Schapiro (55) have argued that this is due to the large number of other factors—social, personal, and genetic—which may affect the course of the disease. This may be true, but if so, the problem should be soluble by increasing the numbers in the RCTs. I am also rather mystified by Roth's and Shapiro's final statement in this section of their article: 'Results from one clinical trial favouring the efficacy of an anti-depressive drug are not invalidated by the negative findings from another equally well-designed trial.' If the word 'necessarily' had been added after 'not' and before 'invalidated' the statement is unexceptional. We all know that if one is working at the 5 per cent level, in 20 trials one will be expected to give discrepant results but as the sentence stands it invites a logical reversal. 'Negative findings in relation to the efficacy of an anti-depressive drug are not invalidated by positive findings from another equally well-designed trial!' I suspect that this rather thin argument in an otherwise excellent article by distinguished contributors is an attempt to conceal the fact that psychiatry has failed to utilize the technique of the RCT.

One sees the same difficulty in the field of mental handicap. The same social trend is moving the handicapped from the large colony to smaller units in the community. In spite of a pioneer trial by Tizard (56) and some excellent observational work by

Kushlick (57) we still lack well-designed controlled trials measuring effect and cost. I would agree that this whole area has been bedevilled by the economic inequality between 'care' and 'cure' (p. 73). It is possible that measurements of 'benefit' will be easier when economic equality is achieved, but there would be no harm in starting to develop these techniques now.

It is I think becoming clear why the scientific renaissance did not take place. Psychiatry in the last twenty years failed to harness those two winds of change, social and psycho-pharmacological, which could clearly have brought so much benefit with them. The psychiatrists have failed to assess quantitatively the problems they inherited in the form of psycho-analysis and psychotherapy. The failure is I believe due to the failure of psychiatry to develop its methods of assessment to meet the needs of a double-blind RCT. I am not saying that it is easy, but I do think that research has not been concentrated sufficiently in this direction.

Present-day psychiatry is therefore in my view basically inefficient in that it encourages the use of therapies, many of which are of unknown effectiveness and which may possibly be dangerous. They have also failed to work out the optimal place of treatment. They have failed to evaluate psycho-analysis and psychotherapy. I was recently accused of 'logical lunacy' when developing this theme at an international meeting by a very distinguished practitioner in this field. I like being called 'logical' and admit to being neurotic, but I cannot agree that colleagues, however distinguished, intelligent, and hardworking, and who obviously believe they are 'doing good', should have a blank cheque to encourage the use of psychotherapy and the administration of psychotrophic drugs without bothering to measure the benefit and cost of what they are doing.

I have few suggestions to make. I would cut the money available for therapy, though reducing the economic inequality between care and cure (p. 73), and increase the grants for well-designed evaluatory research. From a more practical point of view, I would ban the prescription of amphetamines and put a large number of other psychotrophic drugs on a list which could only be prescribed by psychiatric consultants. I do not suggest this because I think consultants know better than GPs which of these drugs will do more good than harm in the long run. I do not think anyone knows, but they may know more about side-effects and, much more importantly, there are fewer consultants than GPs and it will make the prescriptions more difficult to get. Psychiatry, in my view, must be criticized as using a large number of therapies whose effectiveness has not been proven. It is basically inefficient.

6. TWO ASPECTS OF THE ENT WORLD

a. *Tonsillectomy*

Tonsillectomy is now the commonest cause of admission of children to hospital, and although the admission rate is past its peak of popularity it still accounts for about 150,000 admissions per year, with wide variations in rates between the hospital regions. In 1967, for instance, the rate in the Oxford Region was nearly double that in the Sheffield Region. Originally tonsillectomy was acclaimed as a panacea, but its supporters now only claim that it relieves obstruction in a small number of cases, and reduces the frequency of upper respiratory disease and otitis media in others. A small but not negligible mortality is also now generally admitted.

It was hoped that the advent of RCTs would solve the problem but it has not worked out quite like that. The three trials (58, 59, 60) were concerned with children in whom the value of the operation was considered equivocal. Mawson's trial showed an advantage in the tonsillectomized children in attacks of sore throat, tonsillitis, cervical adenitis, and colds. There was no advantage as regards otitis media. McKee on the other hand found a benefit as regards otitis media, while Roydhouse found a decrease in upper respiratory disease as a result of the operation. Taken altogether the evidence, superficially, is in favour of the operation but unfortunately two major criticisms can be made against all three. The first is that the comparison was made between 'operation' and 'no or inadequate medical treatment'. The correct comparison would have been between 'best surgical' and 'best medical'. Had this been done it is reasonable to suppose that the advantages found in favour of the operation would have been decreased. The other criticism refers to the method of collecting the data on which the assessments were made. These inevitably were based on parents' opinions, and as parents knew whether the children had had an operation or not, any bias on their part for or against the operation may have been very important. Direct evidence about parents' attitudes to tonsillectomy seems lacking, but the continuous popularity of the operation suggests that most parents believe that tonsillectomy is a cure for upper respiratory disease in children. It therefore seems probable that parents with a child on the waiting-list for tonsillectomy will tend to exaggerate the frequency and severity of their child's illness, in comparison with the parents of a child who has had the operation. It is thus impossible to exclude the possibility that the favourable results of the trials may have been due to bias.

The present situation is therefore very unsatisfactory. It will probably be some time before a perfect controlled trial, without bias, and with adequate medical treatment, is mounted. At present there seems every reason to limit tonsillectomy to cases of obstruction. No case should be placed on a surgical waiting-list but always referred for medical treatment, and only when this fails after a prolonged trial should the case be sent to the surgeon. This should reduce the number of tonsillectomies to about one-fifth of the present numbers.

b. Hearing-aids for the elderly

In comparison to the exuberant surgery discussed in the last section the service provided by the same ENT departments for the elderly deaf is very different.

The facts are fairly straightforward. Hinchcliffe (61) using pure-tone audiometry in a study of a random sample of a defined population found that 21 per cent of people had a hearing loss greater than 25 decibels. Other surveys using less accurate methods have in general confirmed this (62, 63, 64). The number of elderly people who have actually sought and obtained medical care for hearing difficulty is much less than these figures would lead one to expect. Townsend and Wedderburn, for instance, found that about 6 per cent had a hearing-aid though apparently 30 per cent might have profited from one. Similar results were found in the other surveys.

This discrepancy of nearly a million old people with untreated hearing problems may be due to the old people themselves, their GPs, or the central out-patients' organization. Little is known about the first two possibilities, but there is sufficient known about the third to arouse disquiet. The usual technique is for the patient to be seen by an otologist who, after physical and audiometric examination, refers the patient if necessary to a hearing-aid centre. There are about 100 of these in England. In these there are about 220 audiology technicians, some of whom work in out-patient departments. The number has actually decreased since 1965, which is not surprising. Their salary scale (Whitley Council, 1969) ranges from £300 p.a. for a 16-year-old student to £1,360 p.a. for a chief audiology technician. The British Association of Otolaryngologists commented in 1971 that 'there is insufficient staff to run the present service'. As a result the service is thoroughly unsatisfactory; the premises on average are poor; the lack of staff makes the work at the centre hurried and communication with the patients difficult. After the fitting of the hearing-aid there is in practice no follow-up and one can imagine the difficulties into which old people can get.

The situation in the local authority administrative areas is little better. They have powers under the National Assistance Act of 1948 to provide services for the deaf, and in July 1960 they were placed under duty to provide such services. There are at present 20 social workers for the deaf, and 70 welfare officers for the deaf employed by local authorities in England and Wales. I found it fascinating to discover that training in welfare for the deaf was often combined with a course in theology, since many people entering this work were clerical! No-one would suggest that the quality of life of all old deaf people can be improved by the most comprehensive audiological service, but large-scale screening would undoubtedly reveal very large numbers of people who could be helped. Such surveys are technically possible, but they are clearly contra-indicated until the present service is improved sufficiently to cope not only with the present demand, but also with the expected demand after widespread screening. This does not, however, mean that carefully designed RCTs should not be started to discover which old people benefit from which type of help.

These two aspects of work in ENT (which, of course, excludes a great deal of their work) do I think demonstrate the sort of pressures in the NHS which at present influence allocation of resources. Here we have two therapies which are probably effective in limited spheres: the first (tonsillectomy) is probably effective for only a small percentage of the cases operated on at present and has a definite mortality, but it is an urgent, dramatic therapy and is still rather fashionable. The other (audiological) is probably effective in improving the quality of life in some of a defined group of the population; it is dull, smacks of an LA service, is not nearly as fashionable and serves the elderly. The first is applied inefficiently because it is too widely applied; the latter is applied inefficiently because it is under-applied.

7. MIDWIFERY

Midwifery is an unusually emotive subject, so *a priori* a very high standard of statistical analysis or an experimental approach would not be expected. Even so it is surprising how successive committees have been content to accept trends as something God-given which must be followed, instead of demanding a more rigorous analysis looking into causality.

The general position is that infantile mortality has been falling regularly since 1928 and successive committees have recommended that an ever-increasing percentage of deliveries should take place in hospital, until the most recent report of the Peel Committee (65) suggested that provision be made for all deliveries to take place in hospital. The only quantitative data produced in support of this is given in Table 6.1, which is a copy of their Table 5. As every DPH student knows this sort of correlation is not evidence. There have been other downward trends in a specific mortality which were unrelated to medical interference, for example, tuberculosis before 1948. It is instructive to recast their Table 5 relating maternal and perinatal mortality to mean length of stay in hospital (Table 6.2). One could as wrongly or rightly conclude from this that the shorter the stay the lower the mortality, as that the higher the hospitalization the lower the mortality. In point of fact, if one examines the data from the

TABLE 6.1. *Maternal mortality, perinatal mortality, and institutional confinements, 1955–68 (England and Wales)*

Year	Maternal mortality rate including abortions per 1,000 total births	Perinatal mortality per 1,000 total births	Percentage of confinements in institutions
1955	0·59	37·4	64·3
1956	0·52	36·7	64·3
1957	0·45	36·2	64·3
1958	0·43	35·0	64·1
1959	0·38	34·1	64·2
1960	0·39	32·8	64·7
1961	0·33	32·2	65·6
1962	0·35	30·8	65·9
1963	0·28	29·3	68·2
1964	0·26	28·2	70·1
1965	0·25	26·9	72·5
1966	0·26	26·3	75·0
1967	0·20	25·4	78·9
1968	0·24*	24·7	80·6

*Provisional.

Source. Extracted from Table 5 of the Peel Report (1970) (65).

TABLE 6.2. *Maternal mortality, perinatal mortality, and average length of post-natal stay, 1958–68*

Year	Maternal mortality rate including abortions per 1,000 total births	Perinatal mortality per 1,000 total births	Average length of post-natal stay in NHS hospitals (days)
1958	0·43	35·0	9·6
1959	0·38	34·1	9·3
1960	0·39	32·8	9·0
1961	0·33	32·2	8·4
1962	0·35	30·8	8·1
1963	0·28	29·3	7·8
1964	0·26	28·2	7·4
1965	0·25	26·9	7·2
1966	0·26	26·3	6·9

Source. Extracted from Tables 5 and 23 of the Peel Report (1970) (65).

regions of England and Wales (Tables 4 and 8 in the Peel Report) there is little correlation between high hospitalization rates and low perinatal mortality and Holland, with a confinement rate of 29·0 per cent has one of the lowest perinatal mortality rates in the world.

It seems very thin evidence on which to base a demand for 0·5 beds per 1,000 of the population. What is needed is a series of measurements of the cost and effect of hospitalizing various percentages of confinements. The increasing percentages would include women at decreasing risk. The effect would include not only measurements of maternal and perinatal mortality but also measures of social acceptance. This would enable some sort of a comparison with other demands on the service. Other factors of course would have to be taken into consideration. The Peel Report calls attention to this. 'Infants suffering from mental and physical handicaps who would have died twenty years ago are now surviving in increasing numbers and a substantial proportion of them have multiple defects.' Another factor is the wishes of the mothers themselves which are dealt with rather cavalierly in the report. It would surely have been possible to organize a survey. There remain the two harsh facts that about 20 per cent of these babies are unwanted, and that babies are one of the few products which the world is producing in excess. It could be argued that these are problems to be dealt with by contraception or abortion and are not relevant here, but if sacrifices have to be made in other branches to achieve a small reduction in perinatal mortality then surely they have some relevance?

Another aspect of the report deserves comment. The striking reduction in length of stay, both antenatal and post-natal, is accepted almost without discussion. Previous lengths of hospital stay were almost certainly too long, but surely the problem is to determine the 'optimum' length of stay for uncomplicated cases with adequate social conditions. This may be a long job and it might be better to put the question in a cruder form and ask: 'What is gained by keeping such mothers in more than forty-eight hours?' There does not seem to have been any experimental attempts in this direction so far. Any estimates of the number of beds required is so dependent on getting the length of stay figure correct that the work seems urgent.

The Peel Committee, by its terms of reference, was not required to examine the antenatal service in any detail, but it seems worthwhile raising some general points. This service is basically a multiphasic screening procedure, which, by some curious chance, has escaped the critical assessment to which most screening procedures have been subjected in the last few years and there seems no reason why the same approach that has proved so useful elsewhere should not be used here.

Some aspects of the antenatal service are, of course, well established. The 'Rhesus' examination and the resultant actions are very effective. The evidence about the test for bacteriuria being an effective screening procedure is satisfactory for pregnant women even if not for others. Much more doubtful is the therapeutic use of iron and vitamins. The effect of iron therapy has been fully investigated in non-pregnant women but there seems to have been some 'ethical' bar to RCTs in pregnant women. My general impression is that the emotive atmosphere should be removed and the subject treated like any other medical activity and investigated by RCTs.

These illustrative examples are inevitably selected but they are, I would claim, reasonably representative.

7

A preliminary evaluation

Before moving on to discuss 'Equality' I think a preliminary summing up is indicated. There are facts from history: the desire to treat on the one hand, and the desire to be treated on the other. There is a strong suggestion that the increase in input since the start of the NHS has not been matched by any marked increase in output in the 'cure' section. In the illustrative examples there were strong suggestions of inefficient use of effective therapies, and considerable use of ineffective ones. For me these all point in one direction and justify at least a preliminary diagnosis of the 'nicest possible type of inflation'. We are by now all accustomed to a situation in which trade unions demand increased wages and industry finds it easier to surrender and raise wages and prices rather than argue. The unions then ask for more wages because of the raised prices, etc. The result is that two sections of the community take the rest for an inflationary ride without increasing national productivity. The analogy with the NHS is not exact but strikingly close. The medical inflation differs from the industrial one in that it is not a self-perpetuating vicious spiral. The external factors in the medical case are mainly the pharmaceutical industry, medical research, the mass media, and the lack of applied research.

To diagnose inflation is not, of course, to suggest a cure, and in some ways the medical situation is more difficult to control than the industrial one. No one I am sure can visualize the BMA with its slogan of 'clinical freedom' controlling inflation by controlling the doctors, and the introduction of economic constraints would certainly 'bite' in the wrong places. On the other hand there are scientific techniques generally accepted by the profession, which can tell us which treatments are effective and how efficiently they are being applied. These are very much more powerful weapons than the late, lamented Prices and Incomes Board ever had, so there is hope.

At this stage I want to interpolate a section on my fears about another possible inflation which may be preventable. The Seebohm Committee (66) has argued the case for sociological independence. Only the future can judge their claim. It is possible that the change may help the social administrators and social workers to lose their inferiority complexes and achieve a real professional status. What worries me is that a brand-new profession seems determined to repeat all the mistakes the medical profession has made in the past. I have pointed out the disastrous inflationary effects of the old tradition that there was a bottle of medicine, a pill, an operation, or a holiday to cure every ailment, and the Social Services seem to be evolving exactly in the same unfortunate way as medicine by suggesting that wherever there is a social 'need' a social worker must be appointed whether or not there is any evidence that the social worker can alter the natural history of the social problem. This is depressing enough but there is another factor which makes the situation more serious. The medical profession have now partially accepted studies of error and evaluation, and British doctors have given a warmer welcome to evaluation by RCTs than other national groups of doctors. Social administrators and social workers on the other hand seem rather antagonistic to evaluation. A recent book, for example, on this actual subject is that of Professor Halmos, *The Faith of the Counsellors* (67). I quote (p. 150): 'The certainty of value is not rooted in empirically verified results; it is rather the assurance derived from an unanalysable moral imperative.' Professor Halmos is referring to the work of counsellors, a group which I understand include a wide range of people from psychiatric social workers and social workers at one end to psychotherapies and psycho-analysts at the other. It is therefore a very sweeping claim. When I first read the paragraph I was vividly reminded of two (of my many) past failures. On one occasion I was trying to persuade a senior consultant to participate in an RCT. He told me that the protocol was morally and ethically unacceptable as he knew what the result would be. On another occasion I was trying to persuade a headmaster to randomize caning and detention for boys who were caught smoking. He answered my arguments by claiming that the trial was unnecessary as he always knew which boy should be caned and which should not. I checked as far as I could later and it looked as though his method was simple. He caned them all. I would like to add another quotation from another source, though it also comes from Professor Halmos's book. 'Convinced of the need to help people—perhaps on emotional rather than intellectual grounds—they feel social work is worthwhile whatever the chances of "success" or "improvement". Not depending for its justification on its results; no failure can therefore discredit' (68). Counselling is, of course, only a small part of the work of the social services and it is difficult to judge how typical the views I have quoted are, but there does seem cause for alarm.

As far as I know there have only been two attempts to assess the value of social work. One was only a pilot study. Both compared highly trained with untrained social workers. In neither was any difference found between the effectiveness of the two types of social workers (69, 70). I think I am justified in fearing a severe inflation, which could be prevented by the rapid introduction of a policy of evaluation into the social services.

8

Equality in the health services

In my brief assessment of the preventive and therapeutic side of the NHS I have used effectiveness and efficiency as my yardstick. These are not as yet really applicable to the 'care' side, so I have chosen 'equality' as my main yardstick in this area, although it does, of course, apply to the therapy as well.

'The availability of good medical care tends to vary inversely with the need for it in the population served.' This quotation from Dr Julian Hart's stimulating article (71) represents the polemical approach to the problem of equality in the NHS, and this approach may well be the most effective method in diminishing inequality which I desire as much as he does. I think, however, that his fears about the possible return of medicine to the forces of the market are much exaggerated and I think he stresses the 'social class' type of inequality to the neglect of other types. I think the study of these other types may lead to more immediate improvements than can be hoped for by his approach. At the same time I wish him well.

The possible 'social class' inequalities in the NHS have excited so much interest that it is advisable to deal with them first. There was undoubtedly gross inequality before the introduction of the NHS. The change caused by the NHS, as far as GP consultations are concerned, was measured in the Government's *Surveys of Sickness* from 1945 to 1952. They showed an undoubted increase in the use of GP services by the lower-income groups over this period (72). Since then there have been several surveys relating social class to various indices of use of the NHS. Ann Cartwright (73) asked a sample of 1,800 people how frequently they visited their doctors. Another joint study by the College of General Practitioners and the General Register Office (74) studied the record of seventy-six practices. Douglas and Bloomfield in *Children under Five* (75) give a picture of hospital admissions; Carstairs and others have published an analysis of the Scottish

In-patient Study (76). More recently Ashford and Pearson have published their findings from Exeter (77). Some of these studies can be criticized from the point of view of their incompleteness, others possibly relied too much on memory but they all showed, with some irregularities, and some exceptions for individual diseases and certain age-groups, a marked gradient increasing from social class I to social class V. In general it would appear that the NHS has gone a long way towards reducing 'social class' inequality, but the critics are still dissatisfied. Richard Titmuss thunders and Julian Hart complains and it is sometimes difficult to see what sort of evidence would satisfy them. Presumably if GP consultation rates, standardized by age, sex, and social class corresponded exactly with incidence rates standardized in the same way they would be content, but they seem curiously un-aware how technically difficult such a comparison would be. Our knowledge of 'true' incidence rates by age, sex, and social class is very limited. In addition there is good evidence that consultation and admission rates are influenced by many factors other than social class, such as size of family, marital status, and smoking habits. A most complex analysis would be necessary to test hypotheses about the relationship between incidence, social class, and medical usage rates, and if one achieved all this and found convincing evidence of under-usage or over-usage on the part of certain social classes what could be done about it, apart from writing a paperback or long article for the *Lancet*? Surely priority should be given to finding out which treatments are effective and then ensuring that these treatments are efficiently given to all who need them?

There are, however, other more obvious types of inequality where some action might be taken to reduce it. For example the gross inequalities between regions. Table 8.1 shows the differences between the regions for bed allocations. No comment is really necessary. It all seems grossly unfair. It is possible to put forward an explanation for these odd differences, but the most likely is that they stem from the number of hospital beds that were in the regions when the NHS started, and steps have already been taken to remedy the situation.

A more serious type of inequality appears when different types

TABLE 8.1. *Allocation of hospital in-patient beds per 1,000 population in regional hospital board areas, 1968*

Area	Allocated beds per 1,000 population									
	All specialties	Acute specialties	Medical	Geriatric and chronic sick*	Surgical	Obstetrics and GP maternity†	Psychiatric	Mental illness	Mental handicap and severe mental handicap	Others
England and Wales	9·6	3·2	1·3	9·8	1·5	2·4	4·1	2·8	1·3	0·5
England										
Newcastle	9·2	3·4	1·3	10·1	1·7	2·5	3·8	2·5	1·2	0·4
Leeds	10·4	3·5	1·5	12·5	1·5	2·5	4·4	3·2	1·3	0·5
Sheffield	7·6	2·5	0·9	9·8	1·2	2·1	3·1	2·0	1·1	0·4
East Anglian	8·4	2·5	0·9	10·4	1·2	2·0	3·8	2·8	1·0	0·4
NW Metropolitan	9·9	3·9	1·7	7·2	1·9	2·4	4·0	2·6	1·4	0·7
NE Metropolitan	9·5	3·6	1·6	10·4	1·7	2·7	3·5	2·5	1·0	0·6
SE Metropolitan	9·7	3·4	1·4	8·4	1·6	2·4	3·9	2·6	1·2	0·3
SW Metropolitan	13·5	3·4	1·5	7·2	1·6	2·6	7·8	5·7	2·2	0·8
Oxford	8·1	2·5	1·0	11·4	1·3	2·4	3·1	2·0	1·1	0·7
South-Western	10·7	2·7	1·1	10·7	1·4	2·6	5·1	3·1	2·0	0·8
Birmingham	8·5	2·8	1·2	11·7	1·3	2·2	3·7	2·5	1·2	0·4
Manchester	9·1	3·2	1·3	10·3	1·5	2·7	3·7	2·2	1·5	0·3
Liverpool	10·6	4·5	2·0	8·5	2·1	2·6	4·1	3·5	0·7	0·5
Wessex	8·8	2·4	1·0	8·8	1·2	2·2	4·0	3·1	0·9	0·6
Wales	9·9	3·7	1·5	9·3	1·7	2·8	3·9	2·9	1·0	0·6

Source. Extracted from Table 4.10, *Digest of Health Statistics* (Department of Health and Social Security, 1970).

*Allocated beds per 1,000 population aged 65 and over.

†Allocated beds per 1,000 female population aged 15–44.

of hospitals are compared. Here I am not concerned with quality of treatment but with quality of living. There are many aspects of a hospital; the effectiveness of the treatment, the efficiency with which it is given, the care given by the staff and the basic standard of living of the place. Under the latter I include food, heating, lighting, decoration, and comfort. All doctors and many others have known for years of the growing gap between the standard of living in an acute general hospital on the one hand and psychiatric, geriatric, and mentally deficient institutes on the other. This has been known for a long time but little has been done until very recently. The standard of living has improved in long-stay hospitals, but I suspect the standard of living in district general hospitals has risen even faster as in the world at large where the gap between the rich and the poor countries is increasing. We all mutter (particularly doctors) when we visit wards for the chronic psychiatric or the mentally deficient: 'There, but for the grace of God . . .' Most of us know the probability that we, our relatives, and our friends may end our days in geriatric or psychiatric wards. We all have had ample opportunity to study the figures similar to those in Table 8.2 which have been available for many years, but we (and I include myself) have done practically nothing about it.

The reasons for this marked difference in the standard of living of various types of hospital are not immediately obvious. The longer I stay anywhere the more careful I am about the accommodation. I can put up with practically any hotel for one night, but I am fussy when it comes to two weeks. If the rest of my life came in question I would be very fussy indeed. I know of no official defence of this present state of affairs but I have heard two points made in this context:

1. A district general hospital 'deserves' its 'higher standard of living' because it is more effective than the other types of hospital in altering the natural history of disease and returning people to useful productive work. If the district general hospitals were powerhouses of effective treatment efficiently administered there would be something to be said for this argument, but at present they are not. The only comprehensive follow-up of discharge from an acute general hospital is that of Ferguson (78). He showed

TABLE 8.2. *Cost (£s) per 'in-patient week' for various services in NHS hospitals during the year ended 31 March 1970 in England and Wales*

	Acute (over 100 beds)	Long-stay	Chronic	Maternity	Mental illness	Mental handicap
		Type of hospital				
ENGLAND						
Medical staff	3·10	0·85	0·46	1·94	0·81	0·39
Nursing staff	13·67	9·73	9·55	21·98	6·26	5·28
Domestic staff	2·77	1·62	1·67	4·05	0·60	0·44
Catering	6·07	3·30	2·81	6·06	2·64	2·23
Laundry	1·20	0·78	0·74	1·86	0·40	0·46
Power, light, and heat	1·88	1·29	1·21	2·43	0·88	0·78
Building and engineering maintenance	1·93	1·32	1·01	1·98	1·26	0·97
General cleaning	0·55	0·39	0·32	1·01	0·15	0·13
Net total costs	55·70	25·77	22·50	56·88	17·63	14·96
WALES						
Medical staff	3·00	0·92	0·80	1·09	0·90	0·38
Nursing staff	14·30	11·05	11·94	32·28	6·56	5·73
Domestic staff	2·11	1·99	1·93	2·48	0·57	0·56
Catering	5·81	3·24	3·39	7·22	2·62	2·37
Laundry	1·20	0·76	0·95	2·58	0·37	0·59
Power, light, and heat	2·40	1·80	1·77	3·73	0·86	0·79
Building and engineering maintenance	2·11	1·32	1·34	2·67	1·18	0·92
General cleaning	1·82	1·07	0·84	3·13	0·25	0·19
Net total costs	57·63	29·54	27·97	69·34	18·24	15·50

Source. Extracted from Section 1 of *Hospital Costing Returns 1970* (Department of Health and Social Security and the Welsh Office).

that after two years 36·3 per cent were dead and in all 56·6 per cent unimproved. Even if the suggestion were accepted that district general hospitals are more effective than the other types of hospital, does it necessarily follow that the patients, doctors, nurses, and auxiliaries deserve a higher standard of living than those working in those other hospitals? In the district general hospital the work may be more responsible and more interesting; in the others the work is certainly more tedious and more demanding. The great difficulty of recruiting medical personnel of all kinds for long-stay hospitals makes it clear which type of life such personnel prefer. I do not think the case for district general hospitals 'deserving' a higher standard of living is really established.

2. The second argument runs something like this (though most supporters of the idea do not like formulating it too exactly). The inmates of the long-stay hospitals are not, on average, as sensitive to standards of living as the inmates of district general hospitals. This is almost certainly true since schizophrenics, melancholics, idiots, imbeciles, and senile dements are less sensitive to their environment than the 'acute appendix' and the 'road accident' case, but these represent only a minority of the inmates of long-stay hospitals, and they are 'our brothers and sisters, our cousins and our aunts', and may very likely someday be ourselves.

I think this sort of inequality is the least excusable and the most easily remedied of the many inequalities in the NHS. I give it considerable priority over social class inequality. The historical reasons for its existence, as opposed to the reasons for its continuance, are well known. The chronic hospitals are the direct descendants of the poor-law institutions, while the district general hospitals are the descendants of the voluntary hospitals. The latter were ruled by 'honoraries' who by their ability, wealth, and power in the royal colleges and the ministries saw that the standard of living of the hospitals where they worked kept ahead of the local authority hospitals. There have been great improvements since the NHS took over. In particular, Mr Richard Crossman deserves credit for the way he utilized the 'Ely Hospital' situation to improve the lot of the mentally handicapped, and Sir Keith Joseph is doing an excellent follow-up, but there is still a very great deal to be done. The last report of the NHS Hospital Advisory Service (79) clothes the statistics of Table 8.2 in vivid words if anyone needs further evidence: 'the underprivileged branch of the Health Service'.

There is also the vexed question of inequality due to variation in standard of medical care. This variation undoubtedly exists. There are variations in individual skill, although it is to be hoped that this will be reduced as science replaces opinion and intuition. There is also probably another factor which varies from hospital to hospital. Professor Morris and his co-workers, for instance, have studied inter-hospital variation in case fatality (80). The difference between teaching hospitals and non-teaching hospitals is not unexpected and highly desirable. Teaching hospitals should surely lead their region in all medical matters. Others have interpreted 'quality' differently. They suggest, for instance, that standards can be laid down as to what investigations should be carried out in particular situations. For instance it is not difficult to list all the tests routinely done in some specialized unit in some leading hospital, suggest that they should be done in all district general hospitals and claim that one is improving standards. This seems to me to be inflationary nonsense and merely a medical equivalent of 'keeping up with the Joneses' (or should one in this connection say 'the Thomases'). What one needs here is a measurement of the probability of improved outcome for the patients as each new test is added to the repertoire, together with the cost of each test and its risks.

Finally, one comes to the most important and most interesting type of inequality: inequality between diseases. It is the least discussed of all the 'inequalities' but is, I think, a basic problem of the NHS. The best way of introducing the problem is the division of the medical budget amongst all the medical activities. I suppose some people believe that this is based on complex calculations, using cost/benefit ratios, expected incidence figures, and medical migration rates. I do not actually know how it is done, but I would guess that it would be nearer the truth to describe the process as 'same as last year plus or minus 5 per cent for pressure groups'. This may sound cynical, but what else can administrators do? They lack the necessary information to do much else. At the same time it is well known that there must be some ideal distribution which reduces to a minimum inequality between diseases, or to use economic jargon 'optimizes the output'. What sort of data do we need for this?

Very crudely I think the answer can be put in this way. Let us divide the patient world into broad symptomatic groups: pulmonary, cardiovascular, geriatric, etc. Let us assume that only proven effective treatments are used (except for the conscious use of placebos and a few simple therapies given for 'ethical' reasons). Let us assume that the whole system of diagnosis, therapy, and care is carried out with maximum efficiency. Let us assume a general constraint that all hospitalization is at the same comfort level. The next stage would be to enumerate the various outputs at the present financial level of allocation of money. The outputs will vary from prolongation of life through reduction of morbidity to home and hospital care for those who cannot look after themselves. These outputs (which can, of course, be subdivided *ad infinitum*) will then be costed and calculations made as to how the various outputs could be increased by, say, a 10 per cent increase in financial allocation. Similar calculations would then be made for the screening and preventive services. This, though difficult enough, is a gross simplification as it omits all the constraints due to scarcities of skilled staff, etc.

It was at this stage when I was thinking about the future of the NHS that I used to get stuck. I knew what the next logical step was, but I found it oddly repugnant. My conversion was due to two factors. The first was my slow acceptance of the fact that the process was being done every year unconsciously and inaccurately, and that the process must be better if done consciously. The other factor is the persuasive tongue of Professor Alan Williams of York. He is not responsible for any of my views, but I am very grateful for the time he devoted to me. The process is, of course, the quantification of all the various types of output, i.e. if the saving of a man's life aged 20 and restoring normal expectation of life, is rated as 100, what number should be assigned to the care of a severe schizophrenic? Many people have a reasonable dislike of quantifying value judgements, but I am now convinced it is necessary. I think, although the use of quantification is far ahead, the exercise is worthwhile, if only for the intellectual satisfaction of thinking something through to the end, to demonstrate the incredible difficulties inherent in the two stages, and to determine the direction in which to aim. There are too many enthusiastic economists willing to assume that all medical therapy is 100 per cent effective and 100 per cent efficiently deployed in order to justify their hurry to optimize. I hope they will be discouraged.

9

Conclusions

The main point that I hope emerges from this rapid survey is the existence of the nicest possible type of 'inflation' in the 'cure' sector. I devoted a lot of space to it, because its existence is so little appreciated, but I want to stress the importance of the two other black spots: the marked economic inequality between the 'care' and 'cure' sectors as exemplified by the difference between the different types of hospital and the lack of a proper population policy. Less attention was paid to them because they are already well publicized and I doubted whether any arguments of mine would succeed where others had failed. This does not mean that they are less important; on the contrary, the population problem is by far the most important problem of our time. I want, however, for the moment to consider the three together. I have no intention of joining the clamour for more money for the NHS. If more money becomes available for the welfare services I think an increase in old-age pensions should have priority. In suggesting changes I should therefore argue the case that they will be self-balancing economically, but the prognostic errors of economists urge caution and I shall only attempt it in a very general way. Population control should not be very expensive. Free contraception is unlikely to cost more than can be saved from prescriptions for vitamins and psychotropic drugs and as abortions make less demand on the NHS than childbirth there should be a net gain, unless the number of abortions rises much more steeply than the decrease in births. On the other hand the economic rehabilitation of the 'care' services will need very considerable sums of money both in capital and expenditure and it is this money that we must look for by the scientific control of inflation, and this will not be easy.

The first step in this direction is a marked increase in knowledge through applied medical research. I have already outlined the extent of the work needed in relation to diagnosis and treatment, as well as in the fields of monitoring, record linkage, and operational research, but the organization needed to carry out this research raises very real problems. I have sketched the unhappy history of 'applied' medical research in this country, and the moment of writing (before the Dainton Committee has reported) is not a particularly suitable moment for expressing the worm's-eye view. However I think the MRC does such an excellent job at present on 'purish' medical research that it would be absurd to upset the organization either by splitting it between the Science Research Council and the Department of Health and Social Security, or asking it to take responsibility for applied medical research. It has developed admirable expertise in spotting 'winners' and assessing research protocols sent in from outside. It has been less successful, at any rate in the past, in assessing general medical research priorities for the country, and seeing that they are carried out. Two alternatives to the MRC as organizers of applied medical research have been suggested: an institute of applied medical research and the DHSS itself. The one advantage of an institute is its independence of the executive. In this country there has traditionally been considerable mistrust of departments organizing their own research because it is believed that the usual political and administrative pressures from which departments suffer might jeopardize the independence of the research. On the other hand setting up a new organization, independent of both the MRC and the DHSS, is something surely to be avoided unless there is no other solution. The DHSS, as organizer of applied medical research, has two points in its favour at least. It knows the research priorities of the NHS better than anyone else, although there is scope, I suspect, for an improved organization within the DHSS in this respect. It also, in the last few years, has shown great ability in building up a considerable research department. I have had the good fortune to be in fairly close contact with the research section of the DHSS. I have found its members friendly and efficient and I have seen no trace of political pressure. My only criticisms are that the staff, though able, is numerically very small, and that it is not clear to other research workers that their proposals are objectively assessed, but from what I have seen of the work of the DHSS I think the assessments are very fair. I would, therefore, on balance favour the DHSS being in charge of applied medical research, as long as close liaison is kept with the MRC. Before leaving the problem of central organization I want to make some additional points. There is in the first place a twenty-year backlog of applied research. In the second place 'purish' research can be done and is in fact done all over the world. Applied research to improve the effectiveness and efficiency of our NHS can only be done in this country. It is therefore essential that for a considerable number of years applied research must be given very considerable financial priority. The next problem concerns the people who are going to do this research. There are the universities, MRC units, and the DHSS's own units which are growing in number. Will they suffice? On the whole I doubt it. Medical scientists interested in research are rare and those interested in applied medical research rarer still. Then there is the nature of such research. It is the exact opposite of the classical romantic image where the young scientist suddenly has an idea in his bath, spends the next three weeks frenziedly working out how to test the hypothesis and gets the Nobel prize a year later. In the sort of applied research needed, the hypotheses about effectiveness, place of treatment, length of stay, are readymade. The technique will nearly always be an RCT. The main problems are to find a co-operative group of consultants and GPs and persuade them to adopt a particular protocol and to find bright young medical scientists who enjoy playing these sort of games.

I can make only a few relatively cheerful suggestions. The first is to call attention to the low cost of such RCTs in comparison with the usual 'phenomenological' type of medical research. Secondly, I have some hope of something constructive being organized at 'regional' level.

The Hospital Activity Analysis will presumably continue to be carried on at this level and if the analyses could all have a 100 per cent coverage and an acceptably low error rate, and if, in addition to the present cryptic notes, papers on specific diseases were prepared by medical scientists suggesting the sort of action clinicians should take, and if finally these papers were read and discussed by the corresponding 'Cogwheel' committees something might emerge. Thirdly I have some hope that the royal colleges might help in two ways, by introducing questions about length of stay, place of treatment, etc., into their examinations and by encouraging experience of RCTs in their training programmes for specialists. The Royal Colleges of Physicians are, I think, to be particularly praised in being such a long-suffering midwife to the new Faculty of Community Medicine, but so far my researches have failed to reveal any question on 'length of stay' in the membership examinations. There is also the hope that teaching hospitals, when the supply of money for phenomenological research is reduced, will interest themselves in applied research of value to their region.

The number and quality of departments of social (or community) medicine is increasing, although there are still too few in London, and it is on them that the main responsibility rests to produce enough trained medical manpower to carry through this formidable research programme, and to provide facilities for interested consultants to carry out their own research. It is therefore important that these departments should not be robbed of their teaching staff too quickly in order to build up 'applied' research units either as 'Research and Intelligence' units in the regions, or as independent units under the DHSS. It would be wrong to conclude this section without expressing my opinion that we will never get sufficient medical personnel of the right calibre for this sort of work (and some are essential even though a great deal can be done by non-medical personnel) unless some form of remuneration comparable to the clinicians' merit awards is introduced. I accept the fact that clinical responsibility for the individual is a serious one, but so is the responsibility for the community, but the present ineffectiveness, inefficiency, and lack of equality in the NHS has largely been produced or condoned by the clinical establishment within the NHS and those needed to cure the inflation should be adequately rewarded.

The second problem is the implementation of the research results we can expect from a marked increase in applied medical research inside the NHS and its effects on the medical profession. There will be many such effects but the one I want to discuss is the probable decrease in clinical and administrative freedom. At present the medical profession enjoys very considerable freedom in the NHS. Within very wide limits, the doctors can prescribe as they like, and give as many 'days off' as they wish, and decisions about consultation, admission, operation, and discharge are in their hands. I imagine that if the research results are implemented there will be a considerable limitation of this freedom. Indications for prescriptions, diagnostic tests, admission, length of stay in hospital, etc., will get more and more clearly defined and a sort of 'par for the course' associated with each group of signs and symptoms will be established, and those doctors with too many 'strokes' above or below 'par' will be asked to justify themselves before their peers. The evidence needed will, of course, be the effect on the outcome of the disease. Some will undoubtedly object to this, but if the evidence on which the 'par' is based is made clear and the objective of being fair to all patients served by the NHS is explained I doubt if many will emigrate.

There will also be limitations on the present administrative freedom. Allocations of funds and facilities are nearly always based on the opinions of senior consultants, but, more and more, requests for additional facilities will have to be based on detailed argument with 'hard evidence' as to the gain to be expected from the patients' angle and the cost. Few can possibly object to this.

Yet another freedom, at a different administrative level, will almost certainly disappear. When new types of operations or treatment are introduced to which considerable prestige is attached there is a marked tendency for all teaching hospitals and many others to feel that they must set up such centres, regardless of the number of cases that are likely to require such treatment at that particular hospital. Ideally from the patients' point of view there should be as few centres as is compatible with the demand for the particular treatment. Only in this way can the surgeons and physicians get sufficient experience to make the procedure as efficient as possible, for example, by reduction in operative fatality.

Examples of this misuse of freedom are probably to be seen in open-heart surgery and the implantation of permanent pace-makers. There are, for instance, eighteen London hospitals which undertake open-heart surgery. One does not know how many such operations each hospital carries out, and what the case fatality in each case is, but is it difficult not to conclude that the case fatality rate would probably be lower and that there would be much more efficient use of facilities if this sort of surgery were concentrated in two or three hospitals. The story of permanent pacemakers is rather similar. A survey in 1967 found forty-five hospitals doing this, of which ten did only one implantation in that particular year.

We have still to take a look into the future and see what the NHS would look like if all this research was completed and implemented in order to look at the financial consequences. I see one major change occurring with which several other minor changes are associated. The main change will be the movement of the centre of gravity of medicine from the hospital to the community, associated with a rise in the importance of the GP in relation to the consultant, and the disappearance of the pathologist as the final medical arbiter. He has held that position since the time of Virchow because he could tell the consultant whether his diagnosis was right or wrong. This is a valuable but minor function. He will be replaced by the medical scientist who will measure the effectiveness and efficiency of therapy in the hospital and the community and in conjunction with social scientists assess the adequacy of community care.

The district general hospital will either become smaller or there will be fewer of them. The number of acute hospital beds will probably fall below two per thousand (as suggested by the DHSS's 'Best-Buy Hospitals'). The hospitals will be very intensive. In most cases investigations will be completed before admission and no-one will be admitted unless there is a reasonable probability of effective therapy. Lengths of stay will be very much shorter, partly due to earlier discharge to community hospitals. Out-patient departments will be transformed. There will be very few chronic out-patients as they will be increasingly under the care of their GPs. New out-patients will increasingly be seen in health centres. The usual argument against this is that it is a waste of the consultant's time, which, of course, ignores the waste of patients' time. The theoretical argument runs, 'Unless the consultant's marginal productivity is greater than the sum of that of all his patients the organization of the consultant's time is not identical with the maximization of the community's resources'

(I do like economic jargon when it supports my own prejudices). Another change in out-patient departments will be their increased use for cold surgery and investigations. Assessment by the hospital staff with continuous care by the GP in the community will become the general rule for mental abnormalities, geriatric, and chronic disease in general. Only those requiring very specialized care will be retained in the hospitals.

In the community there will be health centres, community hospitals, and other specialized units providing care near the patients' homes for all the various types of disability. In urban areas a health centre and community hospital will usually be located in the grounds of the district general hospital. The GP of the future, with adequate auxiliaries and working closely with the social services, should have a wonderful chance to organize the complete care of the community. It is to be hoped that he will rise to the opportunity.

Imposed on this different physical set-up (and, of course, partly causing it) will be an increased effectiveness and efficiency. There will be a marked reduction in the use of ineffective remedies and of effective remedies used inefficiently. The cost of diagnostic tests will be much reduced partly by automation and partly by concentrating on tests that lead through diagnosis to effective action. This will all lead to very considerable savings, but the main savings both in capital and running costs will undoubtedly come from the marked reduction in hospital beds in the district general hospital. One must not, of course, expect a straightforward reduction proportional to the number of beds. The hospital of the future will be very intensive, and can be expected to develop some very expensive quirks. There are also snags about reducing length of stay. The reduction of cost is not proportionate to the reduction in the length of stay. Particularly in surgical cases the main cost is incurred in the first few days of hospital stay. The main savings occur when patients receive adequate treatment without admission to hospital. Until we know from the results of RCTs which types of disease can be as well treated at home as in hospital estimates of possible savings are clearly subject to enormous error, but there does seem to be a real hope of saving sufficient money to pay for the economic rehabilitation of the 'care' services.

It is worth considering what will happen if we do not use science to control this inflation. The first results are already visible in the form of the widening gap between the standards in the 'care' sector and the 'cure' sector. It is wide enough at present; to widen it would be a national shame. But if the inflation continues the next step is inevitably the return of much of the 'cure' sector to the forces of the market place, which I do not believe many doctors wish to happen.

My colleagues, in their devotion to their patients, evoke my admiration, but also remind me of Agatha in Eliot's 'The Family Reunion', who wanted action:

> Not for the good that it will do
> But that nothing may be left undone
> On the margin of the impossible

I hope clinicians in the future will abandon the pursuit of the 'margin of the impossible' and settle for 'reasonable probability'. There is a whole rational health service to gain.

SUMMARY

An investigation into the working of the clinical sector of the NHS strongly suggests that the simplest explanation of the findings is that this sector is subject to a severe inflation with the output rising much less than would be expected from the input. The evidence is based on a historical survey, crude input and output measurements, and measurements of effectiveness and efficiency in the diagnosis and treatment of some common diseases. This does not amount to proof, but is reasonably conclusive. It is suggested that the inflation could be controlled by science, in particular by the wide use of randomized controlled trials. It is hoped that by control of inflation in the 'cure' sector enough money will be made available to deal with other black spots in the NHS, such as population control and the economic inequality between the 'cure' and 'care' sectors.

POSTSCRIPT

I feel in this book I may have been too critical of my colleagues for whom I actually have the greatest admiration and affection. I would like to stress that I have been comparing them with an absolute standard. If one adopts a comparative approach I would like to stress how very far ahead the medical profession (particularly in the UK) is of other professions. What other profession encourages publications about its error, and experimental investigations into the effect of their actions? Which magistrate, judge, or headmaster has encouraged RCTs into their 'therapeutic' and 'deterrent' actions? As regards reproducibility let us remember the number of judges who have their judgements reversed on appeal and the diversity of opinion expressed by economists about the Common Market, and as regards 'risk' let us remember the number of bridges that have fallen down.

REFERENCES

1. McKeown, T., and Lowe, C. R. (1966). *An Introduction to Social Medicine*, pp. 3–18 (Oxford: Blackwell Scientific Publications).

2. Daniels, M., and Hill, A. B. (1952). 'Chemotherapy of pulmonary tuberculosis in young adults. An analysis of the combined results of three Medical Research Council trials', *Br. med. J.* 1, 1162.

3. Office of Health Economics (1971). *Off Sick*. OHE Publication no. 36.

4. Palmer, J. W. (1965). 'Smoking, caning and delinquency in a secondary modern school', *Br. J. prev. soc. Med.* 19, 18.

5. Cochrane, A. L., and Springett, V. H. (1968). 'Pulmonary tuberculosis', in *Screening in Medical Care* (Oxford University Press for the Nuffield Provincial Hospitals Trust).

6. Galloway, T. McL. (1963). 'Management of vaccination and immunization procedures by electronic computer', *Med. Offr*, 109, 232.

7. Saunders, J. (1970). 'Results and costs of a computer-assisted immunization scheme', *Br. J. prev. soc. Med.* 24, 187.

8. Royal College of Physicians (1971). *Smoking and Health Now*. A report of the Royal College of Physicians (London: Pitman Medical and Scientific).

9. Mather, H. G., Pearson, W. G., Read, K. L. Q., Shaw, D. B., Steed, G. R., Thorne, M. G., Jones, S., Guerrier, C. J., Eraut, C. D., McHugh, P. M., Chowdhury, N. R., Jafary, M. H., and Wallace, T. J. (1971). 'Acute myocardial infarction: Home and hospital treatment', *Br. med. J.* 3, 334.

10. Universities Group Diabetes Program (1970). 'A study of the effects of hypoglycemic agents on vascular complications in patients with adult-onset diabetes. II. Mortality results', *Diabetes*, 19, suppl. 2.

11. Knatterud, G. L., Meinert, C. L., Klimt, C. R., Osborne, R. K., and Martin, D. B. (1971). 'Effects of hypoglycemic agents on vascular complications in patients with adult onset diabetes', *J. Am. med. Ass.* 217, 6, 777.

12. Elwood, P. C., Waters, W. E., Green, W. J., and Wood, M. M. (1967). 'Evaluation of a screening survey for anaemia in adult non-pregnant women', *Br. med. J.* 4, 714.

13. Waters, W. E. (1970). 'Controlled clinical trial of ergotamine tartrate', ibid. 2, 325.

14. Breast Cancer Symposium (1969). 'Points in the practical management of breast cancer', *Br. J. Surg.* 56, 782.

88

References

15. COCHRANE, A. L., and MOORE, F. (1971). 'Expected and observed values for the prescription of vitamin B12 in England and Wales', *Br. J. prev. soc. Med.* **25**, 3, 147.

16. FARQUHARSON, E. L. (1955). 'Early ambulation with special reference to herniorrhaphy as an out-patient procedure', *Lancet*, **ii**, 517.

17. WEDDELL, J. (to be published).

18. LOGAN, R. F. L., KLEIN, R. E., and ASHLEY, J. S. A. (1971). 'Effective management of health', *Br. med. J.* **2**, 519.

19. HEASMAN, M. A., and CARSTAIRS, V. (1971). 'Inpatient management variations in some aspects of practice in Scotland', ibid. **1**, 495.

20. BLODGETT, J., and BEATTIE, E. (1947). 'The effect of early post-operative rising on the recurrence rate of hernia', *Surg. Gynec. Obstet.* **84**, 716.

21. MORRIS, D., WARD, A. W. M., and HANDYSIDE, A. J. (1968). 'Early discharge after hernia repair', *Lancet*, **i**, 681.

22. ODDIE, J. A., HASLER, J. C., VINE, S. M., and BENNETT, A. E. (1971). 'The community hospital', ibid. **ii**, 308.

23. MEDAWAR, P. B. (1967). *The Art of the Soluble* (London: Methuen).

24. COCHRANE, A. L., and HOLLAND, W. W. (1971). 'Validation of screening procedures', *Br. med. Bull.* **27**, 1, 3.

25. MEDICAL RESEARCH COUNCIL (1966). *Questionnaire on Respiratory Symptoms and Instructions for its Use* (Dawlish, Devon: W. J. Holman).

26. ROSE, G. A. (1962). 'The diagnosis of ischaemic heart pain and intermittent claudication in field surveys', *Bull. Wld Hlth Org.* **27**, 645.

27. FLETCHER, C. M. (1952). 'The clinical diagnosis of pulmonary emphysema —An experimental study', *Proc. R. Soc. Med.* **45**, 577.

28. LEWIS, S. M., and BURGES, B. J. (1969). 'Quality control in haematology: Report of interlaboratory trials in Britain', *Br. med. J.* **4**, 253.

29. ELWOOD, P. C., and PITMAN, R. G. (1966). 'Observer error in the radiological diagnosis of Paterson–Kelly webs', *Br. J. radiol.* **39**, 587.

30. MIALL, W. E., and OLDHAM, P. D. (1958). 'Factors influencing arterial blood pressure in the general population', *Clin. Sci.* **17**, 3, 409.

31. COCHRANE, A. L., and GOLDBERG, A. (1968). 'A study of faecal porphyrin levels in a large family', *Ann. hum. Genet.* **32**, 195.

32. ELWOOD, P. C., and WOOD, M. M. (1966). 'The effect of oral iron therapy on the symptoms of anaemia', *Br. J. prev. soc. Med.* **20**, 172.

33. KEEN, H., CHLOUVERAKIN, C., JARRETT, R. J., and BOYNS, D. R. (1968). 'The effect of treatment of moderate hyperglycaemia on the incidence of arterial disease', *Postgrad. med. J.*, Suppl. 44, 960.

34. GRAHAM, P. A. (1968). 'Definition of pre-glaucoma: a prospective study', *Trans. Ophthal. Soc., U.K.* **88**, 153.

References

35. HAMILTON, M., THOMPSON, E. N., and WISNIEWSKI, T. K. M. (1964). 'The role of blood pressure control in preventing complications of hypertension', *Lancet*, **i**, 235.

36. VETERANS ADMINISTRATION CO-OPERATIVE (1967). 'Study group on anti-hypertensive agents', *J. Am. med. Ass.* **202**, 1028.

37. —— (1971). 'Study group on anti-hypertensive agents', ibid. **213**, 1143.

38. CARMALT, M. H. B., and WHITEHEAD, T. P. (in press). *Proc. R. Soc. Med.*

39. GURNEY, C., HALL, R., HARPER, M., GRIFFITH OWEN, S., and ROTH, M. (1970). 'Newcastle thyrotoxicosis index', *Lancet*, **ii**, 1275.

40. DAWSON, J. J. Y., DEVADATTA, S., FOX, W., RADHARKRISHNA, S., RAMAKRISHNAN, C. V., SOMASUNDARAH, P. R., STOTT, H., TRIPATHY, S. P., and VELU, S. Tuberculosis Chemotherapy Centre, Madras (1966). 'A five year study of patients with pulmonary tuberculosis—a current comparison of home and sanatorium treatment for 1 year with isoniazid plus P.A.S.', *Bull. Wld Hlth Org.* **34**, 533.

41. TUBERCULOSIS SOCIETY OF SCOTLAND (1960). 'The treatment of pulmonary tuberculosis at work: a controlled trial', *Tubercle. Lond.* **41**, 161.

42. SPRIGGS, E. A., BRUCE, A. A., and JONES, M. (1961). 'Rest and exercise in pulmonary tuberculosis; A controlled study', ibid. **42**, 267.

43. TYRELL, W. F. (1956). 'Bed rest in the treatment of pulmonary tuberculosis', *Lancet*, **i**, 821.

44. THOMAS, H. E., FORBES, D. E. P., LUNTZ, G. R. W. N., ROSS, H. J. T., MORRISON SMITH, J., and SPRINGETT, V. H. (1960). '100 per cent sputum conversion in newly diagnosed pulmonary tuberculosis', ibid. **ii**, 1185.

45. CROFTON, J. (1959). 'Chemotherapy of pulmonary tuberculosis', *Br. med. J.* **1**, 1610.

46. PANDE, B. R., MARTISCHNIG, K. M., and FEINMANN, L. (1970). 'A two-year follow-up of 181 sputum-positive tuberculosis patients treated in Gateshead between 1961 and 1966', *Tubercle*, **51**, 39.

47. LONDON SCHOOL OF HYGIENE AND TROPICAL MEDICINE (1971). Unpublished thesis. Personal communication.

48. METROPOLITAN LIFE INSURANCE CO. (1969). *Statist. Bull.* **50** (December), 1.

49. INTERNATIONAL ANTICOAGULANT REVIEW GROUP (1970). 'Collaborative analysis of long-term anticoagulant administration after acute myocardial infarction', *Lancet*, **i**, 203.

50. MEDICAL RESEARCH COUNCIL WORKING PARTY ON THE TREATMENT OF MYOCARDIAL INFARCTION (1968). 'Potassium, glucose and insulin treatment for acute myocardial infarction', ibid. **ii**, 1355.

51. HOFVENDAHL, S. (1971). 'Influence of treatment in a coronary care unit on prognosis in acute myocardial infarction', *Acta Med. Scand.*, Suppl. 519.

52. PANTRIDGE, J. F., and GEDDES, J. S. (1967). 'A mobile intensive-care unit in the management of myocardial infarction', *Lancet*, **ii**, 271.

References

53. REID, D. D., and EVANS, J. G. (1970). 'New drugs and changing mortality from non-infectious disease in England and Wales', *Br. med. Bull.* **26**, 3, 191.

54. LEYBURN, P. (1967). 'A critical look at antidepressant drug trials', *Lancet*, **ii**, 1135.

55. ROTH, M., and SHAPIRA, K. (1970). 'Social implications of advances in psychopharmacology', *Br. med. Bull.* **26**, 3, 197.

56. TIZARD, J. (1966). *Survey and Experiment in Special Education* (University of London).

57. KUSHLICK, A. (1967). 'A method of evaluating the effectiveness of a community health service', *Soc. and Econ. Admin.* **4**, 29.

58. MAWSON, S. R., ADLINGTON, P., and EVANS, M. (1967). 'A controlled study evaluation of adeno-tonsillectomy in children', *J. Laryngol.* **81**, 777.

59. McKEE, W. J. E. (1963). 'A controlled study of the effects of tonsillectomy and adenoidectomy in children', *Br. J. prev. soc. Med.* **17**, 49.

60. ROYDHOUSE, N. (1969). 'A controlled study of adenotonsillectomy', *Lancet*, **ii**, 931.

61. HINCHCLIFFE, R. (1961). 'Prevalence of the commoner ear, nose and throat conditions in the adult rural population of Great Britain', *Br. J. prev. soc. Med.* **15**, 3, 128.

62. SHELDON, J. H. (1948). *The Social Medicine of Old Age* (Oxford University Press for the Nuffield Foundation).

63. WILLIAMSON, J., STOKOE, I. H., GRAY, S., FISHER, M., SMITH, A., McGHEE, A., and STEPHENSON, E. (1964). 'Old people at home: their unreported needs', *Lancet*, **i**, 1117.

64. TOWNSEND, P., and WEDDERBURN, D. (1965). *The Aged in the Welfare State* (London: G. Bell and Sons).

65. DEPARTMENT OF HEALTH AND SOCIAL SECURITY (WELSH OFFICE) (1970). *Domiciliary Midwifery and Maternity Bed Needs.* Report of the sub-committee (Peel Report) (London: HMSO).

66. SEEBOHM REPORT (1968). *Report of the Committee on Local Authority and Allied Personal Social Services*, Cmnd. 3703 (London: HMSO).

67. HALMOS, P. (1965). *The Faith of the Counsellors*, p. 150 (Letchworth: Garden City Press).

68. RODGERS, B. N., and DIXON, J. (1960). *Portrait of Social Work*, p. 155 (London: Oxford University Press).

69. WATERS, W. E., COCHRANE, A. L., and COLLINS, J. (to be published). 'Evaluation of social therapy in chronic alcoholism.'

70. GOLDBERG, E. M. (1970). *Helping the Aged* (London: Allen and Unwin).

71. HART, J. T. (1971). 'The inverse care law', *Lancet*, **i**, 405.

72. LOGAN, W. P. D., and BROOK, E. M. (1957). *Survey of Sickness, 1943–1952.* GRO Studies on Medical and Population Subjects no. 12 (London: HMSO).

References

73. CARTWRIGHT, A. (1967). *Patients and their Doctors* (London: Routledge and Kegan Paul).

74. LOGAN, W. P. D. (1960). *Morbidity Statistics from General Practice*. GRO Studies on Medical and Population Subjects no. 14 (London: HMSO).

75. DOUGLAS, J. W. B., and BLOOMFIELD, J. M. (1958). *Children under Five* (London: Allen and Unwin).

76. CARSTAIRS, V., and PATTERSON, P. E. (1966). 'Distribution of hospital patients by social class', *Hlth Bull. (Edinb.)*, **24**, 59.

77. ASHFORD, J. R., and PEARSON, N. G. (1970). 'Who uses the health services and why?', *Jl R. statist. Soc. A*, **133**, 295.

78. FERGUSON, T., and MACPHAIL, A. N. (1954). *Hospital and Community* (Oxford University Press for the Nuffield Provincial Hospitals Trust).

79. DEPARTMENT OF HEALTH AND SOCIAL SECURITY (WELSH OFFICE) (1971). *National Health Service Hospital Advisory Service—Annual Report 1969-70* (London: HMSO).

80. LIPWORTH, L., LEE, J. H., and MORRIS, J. N. (1963). 'Case fatality in teaching and non-teaching hospitals 1956-59', *Medical Care*, **1**, 71.

92

Some reflections

The invitation to write a Rock Carling prize essay about the Health Service came by telephone. I was talking to Dr R. H. L. Cohen at the time and, as usual in his company, was slightly euphoric. As a result I accepted. In cold blood I would almost certainly have refused—and quite rightly. I knew far too little about health services; I had too little experience of clinical work and medical administration and above all I was, as Professor, Director, and chronic Committee member, far too busy. But owing to Dick Cohen's persuasive powers I accepted. It led to some unseemly delays, a lot of writing between 11 pm and 3 am, and an increased consumption of whisky.

The title deserves a note. Neither Nuffield nor I liked it, but we couldn't think of anything else. In retrospect it should have been called 'So much goes in . . .' (The comparison between the NHS and the crematorium was the most popular passage in the book.) The title also caused real trouble in certain countries. When lecturing in Brussels to a large WHO audience, with multilingual translation, a section of the interpreters went on strike and held up the meeting for about two hours because I used the word 'efficiency'. The interpreters involved with the French language argued that there was only one word in French for 'effectiveness' and 'efficiency': 'efficacité'; that French was a perfect language and therefore I must be talking nonsense (although they admitted they understood my definitions perfectly). I offered 'efficience' as a word widely used in French engineering, but it was turned down as 'Franglais' as opposed to 'Français'. The same difficulty appears in other languages, such as Danish: and even the Americans have let me down by using 'efficacity' instead of 'effectiveness'. Oddly enough, I was allowed to use 'efficience' in French Canada.

Turning now to criticism, may I thank the critics for, in general, being so kind, and the minority for being so irrelevant. I am not ashamed of my ignorance of sociological theory. I am not ashamed

93

of trying to improve a small part of the world, although the world as a whole is imperfect. Some other criticism was certainly true. The book could certainly have been written ten years before—on the basis of my own remarks. But no one had done it or asked me to do it. There were also serious omissions; although I never claimed to be comprehensive. One is my lack of reference to 'monitoring'. Fortunately the gap has been most comprehensively filled by Sir Richard Doll in his lectures. I have nothing to add to his words, except to underline the problem of the effectiveness of monitoring. Monitoring can be very expensive and it should be validated in the usual way, if it is possible. In general it is hoped that monitoring will be effective in improving clinical and administrative decisions and in stimulating research. Can we be sure that all monitoring really has one of these effects? To take an example: Hospital Activity Analysis is generally believed to be more accurate and efficient in Scotland than elsewhere. Is 'length of stay' decreasing more rapidly in Scotland than in other parts of the UK? And if so, is this desirable in the absence of detailed knowledge of optimum length of stay from the patients' point of view? It is possible that the recent spate of randomized controlled trials on length of stay on IHD cases were stimulated by the publication of the extraordinary between-clinician variation in length of stay for this condition, but even if this were true, do we need continuous HAA? I must repeat that I do not want to decry the idea of monitoring. I merely want a more critical attitude towards the effectiveness of each type of monitoring, less we drift into the situation of monitoring for the sake of monitoring.

Another valid criticism was my neglect of any discussion of quality. The explanation is simple. I find the subject so complex and it has such strong emotional associations for me that the section on quality was not finished in time. One of the incidents in my own life which helped to delay the writing of that section occurred when I was a POW. I was faced by a ghastly medical problem. I had a young Soviet POW patient dying in great pain. He was making a fearful noise in a large ward. I had no drugs or side ward. No one could talk Russian. In despair, and purely instinctively, I sat on his bed and took him in my arms. The effect was almost magical; he quietened at once and died peacefully a few hours later. I was still with him, half asleep and very stiff. I believe that by personal intervention I improved the quality of care dramatically in this case, and I know it was based on instinct and not on reason. I feel therefore rather diffident about a rational discussion about quality. We all recognize quality when we see it and particularly when we receive it. In 'cure' outcome plays an important part in determining quality, but it is certainly not the whole story. The really important factors are kindliness and ability to communicate on the part of all members of the medical team. In 'care' of course the latter two become very much more important. But what can we do about it? We attempt to teach medical students psychology and sociology, but will we really make them kindlier? We desperately need a test which we could apply to aspirant medical students which would tell us whether they would remain kindly in middle age; but I am advised that the development of such a test is very improbable.

The book has been far more popular than I ever dreamed. Though not approaching the world-wide success of Sir Richard Doll's book in the same series, it has been translated into Polish, Spanish, and Italian and has been widely 'xeroxed' in the US! I found the book's popularity in the US hard to understand. It is possibly explained by a remark made by an American when introduced to me: 'So you're Archie Cochrane. I bought 50 copies of your book as Xmas cards last year.'

The effect on myself is hard to judge; so much else was changing at the same time. I became, unexpectedly, President of the Faculty of Community Medicine in the same week as the book was published. I was also slowly organizing my retirement. But the success of the book undoubtedly gave me great pleasure, and an opportunity through lecturing and travel to 'sell' views that I think are important.

There were two side-effects. Through a feeling of having got away with murder, I became a serious student of health services literature, all the way from Donabedian to Ivan Illich. (I can't say I enjoyed it, but I no longer feel I'm skating on thin ice.) The other effect depressed me. After the publication of the book, the medical world forgot my work on pneumoconiosis and common diseases in the Rhondda Fach. I believe I did my best work there and I'm sorry to see it forgotten, but I suppose one can't have it both ways.

Two great, and I fear somewhat undeserved, honours came to me almost directly through the book: the 'Dunham' lectures at Harvard and an honorary degree at York. My debt to Nuffield is very great indeed.

The effect, if any, of the book is hard to judge as it was published during a period of rapid change. The extent of this change was brought home to me by lectures I gave in Cardiff, one in 1968 and the other this year. They were both concerned with cervical cytology. In the first one I concluded that there was no hard evidence as yet that cervical cytology screening had lowered the death-rate from cancer of the cervix. This produced an uproar with banner headlines attacking me in South Wales newspapers, abusive letters (some anonymous), and no colleague in Cardiff could be found to defend this 'dangerous heretic'. This year I concluded a similar lecture in Cardiff by arguing that we would never know whether cervical smears were effective or not. This was followed by a very unemotional discussion as to whether our present position, in encouraging such screening, was ethically justifiable, and even the practicalities of a randomized controlled trial (which would be very difficult) were calmly discussed.

There are of course many other signs of this change. The improved status of community physicians, the increased acceptability by clinicians of the randomized controlled trial technique and the acceptance in the US of the idea of PSRO. If one looks at individual fields, although there have been great advances there could have been so much more. For instance, in the cardiovascular world there has been the striking (though much delayed) recognition of the need for RCTs in the treatment of slightly raised blood pressure. This is of great importance but it is to be hoped that in this prospect of chemically prolonged life with all its side effects the interesting paper describing an RCT of the effect of relaxation will not be forgotten.

The cardiovascular world also deserves credit for the series of papers randomizing the length of time before mobilization and discharge after IHD attacks. These are outstanding and an example to all other branches of medicine, but how does one relate this activity to the conspiracy of silence which greeted Mather's first paper comparing treatment at home for IHD cases with that in coronary care units? There has really been no reply. Surely, if one feels such trials are unethical, there was scope for a carefully controlled observational study? It is particularly interesting that the main criticism of Mather's trial is that his population was selected in the sense that only 31 per cent of the incident cases were randomized. No one, as far as I know, has succeeded in randomizing all the incident cases falling within the medical definition. Mather is unique in telling us what happened to the cases that were not randomized. The same criticism would apply, to a greater extent, to the American Veterans' blood pressure trials, whose results have been widely accepted. There is a touch of schizophrenia in the cardiovascular world at present. Their reaction to Mather's second paper should be carefully studied by the psychiatrists!

Again there is evidence of the orthopaedic surgeon's lack of reaction to an RCT which established the value of oral anticoagulants for patients with fractures of the femoral neck. Professor J. R. A. Mitchell of Nottingham, in a note attached as an addendum to this chapter, has drawn the group's attention to a situation in which, although the beneficial effect of prophylactic treatment was clearly demonstrated sixteen years ago, a recent survey showed that only 3 per cent of surgeons routinely prescribed anticoagulants.

The responsibility for establishing the causes of this seeming disregard of trials of treatment for IHD cases and for fractures of the femoral neck can hardly be willingly surrendered by the profession to others. Discussion could well, in view of the significance of such trials for the quality of patient care, extend to the question whether it is sufficient that they should depend upon sporadic initiatives.

Space forbids a detailed examination of each medical area but in general I would suggest that priorities for research in the general applied area should be aimed:

1. To prevent the introduction of new drugs and therapeutic procedures unless they are more effective (or equally effective and cheaper) than existing therapies.

2. To evaluate all existing therapies (accepting present constraints), slowly excluding those shown to be ineffective or too dangerous.

3. To determine the optimum place of treatment for those therapies about which there is any doubt.

4. To determine optimum lengths of stay where hospital admission is necessary.

As regards diagnosis, which is costing us so much with so little evidence of effect, the problem is more difficult, because of the efficiency of relating the value of tests to outcome. This, of course, has led to the widespread belief that diagnosis is an end in itself. Several ingenious statistical solutions have been proposed as to how the general problem could be solved—in time. Some progress has been made in reducing the number of tests required to reach the 'correct' diagnosis (although there is usually little evidence that this improves outcome), but the problem is urgent (and our present economic situation so depressing) that I would like to suggest a more rapid crude approach.

The basic idea is that a crude value of a clinical test can be measured by the product of two probabilities:

1. The probability that the result of the test will alter the clinician's therapy.

2. The probability that the alteration in the therapy initiated by the clinician as a result of the test will alter the natural history of the disease for the better.

The interesting point about this approach is that the first probability can be measured reasonably accurately from retrospective data. We may need to do some trials to measure the second probability, but some data may be already available. I admit, however, that I am relying heavily on the astronomical probabilities revealed by the first one to control the present inflationary diagnostic situation. (I admit this approach excludes the value of excluding other treatable disease, the limited value of diagnosing untreatable disease and the value of excluding legal reprisals.)

In conclusion, as regards 'prospect' I think there has been some improvement (which is almost certainly unassociated with anything I have said or published), but it certainly isn't fast enough. In spite of the Rothschild reorganization, the shift in medical research from 'pure' to 'applied' and from 'process' to 'outcome' has not really happened. Possibly our present economic difficulties will supply the necessary stimulus. I remain, illogically, vaguely optimistic. We have the most cost-effective health service in the world and we have all the skills needed to improved it, so (in Masefield's words):

> I have seen good deeds done—by men with
> ugly faces,
> and flowers grow in stoney places,
> So I trust too.

I hasten to add that I do not wish to suggest that my medical and statistical colleagues are less well favoured facially than the average of the population.

Obituary

Professor A. L. Cochrane, who had been director of the Medical Research Council's epidemiology unit in Cardiff and was the first president of the Faculty of Community Medicine, died on 18 June.

Archibald Leman—Archie—was born on 12 January 1909 in Galashiels. He won scholarships, first to Uppingham and then to King's College, Cambridge, where he obtained a first in both parts of the natural science tripos. He graduated MB, BCh late (in 1938) after studying at University College Hospital, London. At first, like many of his generation, he was bemused by Freud and Marx. Unlike most of them he spent a year as a medical student with the International Brigade during the Spanich civil war and started a training analysis in Vienna. Unconvinced by either experience he returned to medical research and then joined the Royal Army Medical Corps in 1940. He was captured in Crete in 1941 (an event that he usually blamed on Evelyn Waugh, the intelligence officer of D Battalion 'Layforce') and spent four years as a prisoner of war in Crete, Greece, and Germany, treating chiefly Soviet, French, and Yugoslav prisoners with tuberculosis. In 1945 he was awarded the MBE for his services as a prisoner of war medical officer.

In 1946 he was given a Rockefeller fellowship, which enabled him to take the DPH at the London School of Hygiene and Tropical Medicine, and spent a year in the United States studying the epidemiology of tuberculosis. On his return he joined the MRC's pneumoconiosis research unit, which had just been set up, as epidemiologist and x ray film reader. There the next 10 years were probably the most productive of his life. With an almost obsessional interest in reproducibility, low rates of refusal, and validation he showed that measurements could be made on populations defined geographically with about the same known inaccuracy as measurements made in laboratories. This helped to make epidemiology a quantitative science but had many other results, notably in pneumoconiosis among coalminers and the epidemiology of bronchitis, anaemia, and rheumatoid arthritis and, later, health service research. In 1957 he survived a professor of surgery's prognosis that he had only three months to live.

He was, possibly unnecessarily, upset by the MRC's decision to hand over research on pneumoconiosis among coalworkers to the National Coal Board with limited participation from the MRC and finally became David Davies professor of chest diseases at the Welsh National School of Medicine and honorary director of the MRC's epidemiology unit. He was not a real success as a professor, either as a teacher or on the senate, though his kindness to students was proverbial, but it gave him a sort of breathing space to switch the direction of his research from epidemiology to health services research. He managed to break through by his evaluation of screening procedures (for glaucoma and anaemia).

He retired as a professor in 1969 to become a full time MRC director, in this second productive period emphasising the importance of discovering, by means of randomised clinical trials, the optimum place of treatment and the optimum length of stay. In 1971 the Nuffield Provincial Hospitals Trust published his book *Effectiveness and Efficiency: random reflections on health services*, which, although undoubtedly lucky in its timing, had a widespread international effect. At the same time he accepted the job of being the first president of the Faculty of Community Medicine. It was rather out of character: he did it in a crisis out of a sense of duty, but it upset his research plans. He managed a difficult important job with competence and achieved what was needed.

He retired to what looked like an Indian summer, living in a three generation household at Rhoose; he completed 20 year follow up studies of the communities he had studied in the 1950s, travelled widely, and studied the health services of developed countries. It did not work out as he hoped, but he continued his research work after some severe setbacks, completing a 30 year follow up study of men in Rhondda in 1983.

He had many other interests and abilities at different ages. He showed above average competence at rugby football, squash, tennis, and skiing and enjoyed collecting pictures and sculptures and gardening. A small volume of his verse exists, written while he was a prisoner of war. He entertained generously, particularly foreign visitors, and always admitted the value of a private income in helping his career.

Another aspect of his life was the support he gave his unfortunate family, chiefly by diagnosis and seeing that they got the best treatment and care. There were 11 in his immediate family: three had porphyria, three severe diabetes, and one juvenile rheumatoid arthritis.

He was a man with severe porphyria who smoked too much and was without consolation of a wife, a religious belief, or a merit award—but he didn't do so badly.

ALC